ED PARKER'S
ENCYCLOPEDIA OF KENPO

Books authored by Ed Parker:

• Kenpo Karate - Law of the Fist and the Empty Hand

• Secrets of Chinese Karate

• Ed Parker's Basic Booklet

• A Woman's Guide to Self Defense

• Ed Parker's Guide to the Nunchaku

• Inside Elvis

• Infinite Insights into Kenpo Volume 1
     Mental & Physical Stimulation

• Infinite Insights into Kenpo Volume 2
     Physical Analyzation I

• Infinite Insights into Kenpo Volume 3
     Physical Analyzation II

• Infinite Insights into Kenpo Volume 4
     Mental & Physical Constituents

• Infinite Insights into Kenpo Volume 5
     Mental & Physical Application

• The Zen of Kenpo
     Meaningful Quotes from the Teachings of Ed Parker

• Ed Parker's Kenpo - Belt Manuals Version 1.0 & 2.0

• Ed Parker's Encyclopedia of Kenpo

ED PARKER'S
ENCYCLOPEDIA OF KENPO

VERSION 1.0

developed and written by
Ed Parker, Sr.

DELSBY

PUBLICATIONS

Library of Congress Cataloging-in-Publication Data

Parker, Edmund K., Sr.
Ed Parker's Encyclopedia of Kenpo
version 1.0

Printed in the United States of America
Library of Congress Catalog Card Number Pending
First Printing August, 1992

ISBN 0-910293-12-0 (SOFT COVER)
ISBN 0-910293-13-9 (HARD COVER)

Edited by
Dave Rolph

Production, Photography, Illustrations,
Cover and Book Design by
Ed Parker, Jr.

DELSBY
PUBLICATIONS
DELSBY PUBLICATIONS
Pasadena, California

Table of Contents

Dedication

Edmund Kealoha Parker, Sr.

*I*n loving memory of a great man, we'll remember you. . .

Acknowledgments

The task of this book has been monumentous, however it had truly been a labor of love. Well over 30 years were spent upon the development of this book, a true accomplished dream of the late Ed Parker. Now a reality come true.

The Ed Parker Estate, would like to express our deepest gratitude to the following people for their assistance with the completion of this book. Thank you, Skip Hancock (what could we have done without you?), and David Sites, for the many hours invested in editing this text and to Dave Rolph for this finished version. Thank you, Charles Gonzales and Castle Lithograph for providing professional printing and extended deadlines. Also thanks goes to Tommy Chavies for all your sleepless nights and dedicated loyalty, not to mention our wonderful production and photo staff Sheri, Larry and Woody, plus our diligent Kenpo models Tommy Chavies, Sean C. Hill, William Kongaika, Tina Martin, Scott Masterson, Tori Norton, Harry Sanders and Chris Woodhouse. Appreciation to Miles Nishi, Aldo Mantano, Robin Woodhouse, Beth Parker Uale, Silvia Parker and Niel Chadwick for last minute assistance. A final thank you to the many individuals who have assisted in this endeavor and were not listed but are greatly appreciated. We could not have finished this publication without you!

Preface

*T*his material was created and written by the late Edmund Kealoha Parker, Sr., Senior Grandmaster and founder of American Kenpo Karate. Mr. Parker was called the "Father of American Karate" and spent over 40 years in the Martial Arts. A true legend in his own time, Mr. Parker's genius and accomplishments were known worldwide by hundreds of thousands of students, instructors, followers and admirers.

On December 15, 1990, in Honolulu Hawaii, Mr. Parker sadly passed away at the untimely age of 59. Prior to his death, Mr. Parker had upgraded, categorized, labeled and defined, movements, concepts, principles and terminology pertaining to American Kenpo. These insights and discoveries may also be applied to other Martial Arts Systems as well. For centuries these movements were left undefined, and were sometimes referred to as "secrets" and or "chi." However, Mr. Parker saw the need to analyze and define motion. His discoveries aid many individuals to find within themselves tremendous speed, power and spectacular results from defensive as well as offensive moves. The success stories resulting from Mr. Parker's monumental work are seemingly endless.

American Kenpo was invented by Mr. Parker, however he was never found to refer to Kenpo as *"his"* art but rather *"our"* art. He always treated it as an entity that grew steadily as a result of peoples' interest in it. As American Kenpo grew, Mr. Parker not only fed his own insights into Kenpo, but his students' as well. He was drawn to perpetuate the Art and encouraged others to do the same. Keeping an open mind is the only way that the Art can grow. As you read Mr. Parker's writings be mindful that these definitions can be interpreted in many ways. Just as *"light"* can refer to either "minimal weight" or "illumination", so must you search for other meanings contained within these writings. The terminology found within this book is not cast in cement, but is a guideline to aid practitioners to gain maximum efficiency from their training. It is also a beginning for American Kenpo, not an ending; and this why this book is referred to as version 1.0. Hopefully in the future, as Kenpo grows, there will be space for new versions of this publication. A **NOTES** section is included within this book to encourage defining new terminology.

Working with my father throughout the years I experienced so many insights. I remember him once saying *"you know son, after all the years I've spent working with Kenpo, I finally realize that what I know is nothing compared to what there is to learn."* I saw him reach a new level of awareness. Ed Parker was a student to the very end. May we all share in boundless thirst for knowledge, as we continue his work, and study his teachings.

On behalf of the Parker family we wish you much success learning, teaching and perpetuating the values found within Kenpo. Most of all enjoy our father's work.

- *Ed Parker, Jr.*

Introduction

*F*rom my first day of training I was fascinated by Kenpo, its unique nature keeping my curiosity aroused, and whetting my appetite for further knowledge. Examining the contents of each lesson, I was intrigued with the what, how, and why of it all. As I analyzed what I was taught, I became aware of the personal pros and cons of each of the moves. It was obvious that tailoring the moves to an individual's requirements made the difference between those moves being applicable, or not. Each lesson increased my knowledge of motion, and the many facets that made up the total structure. While I approved of what I was learning, I disapproved of the arbitrary sequential order of executing those moves. Because I was interested in employing logic to what I was doing, I disapproved of the ineffectual employment of motion which I felt could invite unwanted problems. The more I pursued Kenpo knowledge, the more I became dissatisfied with conventional answers. As I dissected motion, I reaffirmed my belief that logic was the key ingredient influencing consistent and organized methods of study. Through structuring my work like medical and other scientific disciplines, I achieved greater clarity, and the ability to continually modify and update my newly discovered concepts, theories, and principles.

After years of experimenting, discovering, teaching, and sharing, my efforts have culminated in a distinctive method of converting verbal language into physical language. I try to personalize the lessons through the use of analogies, sayings, and short stories, making real for most students what are often "too technical" descriptions. After considering the techniques and principles in light of their own experience, students achieve a greater understanding of Kenpo and what its applications mean for them.

Kenpo's scientific structuring and its personalized teaching methods have allowed it to expand unilaterally. This expansion has resulted not only in a generation of new concepts, but in a new and equally growing vocabulary as well. I have tried to develop the terminology of Kenpo utilizing the same methods with which I teach. Drawing from the same well as other scholars, I have attempted to personalize the terminology by using words that have universally pictorial connotations (Anchoring, Begging Hands, Web of Knowledge, etc.). Once visualized, the concepts are more easily understood physically. As these terms, definitions, and applications are absorbed on a visual and physical plane, through diligent practice they become ingrained, and the students response becomes instinctive and extemporaneous.

I admonish you to study the contents of this book, and make learning a delightful experience. Allow Kenpo to be your second language if you are not already bi-lingual. Master the Kenpo language, and expand your knowledge beyond your expectations. Most importantly, remember that this language of motion, once physically ingrained, and internalized, can save your life.

- Ed Parker, Sr.

X

The Encyclopedia

ACCELERATED MOVES - (1) Moves that are advanced in context. These moves are taught to the more adept, who soon learn to apply them with precision and sophistication. (2) Rapid moves that gain momentum with each additional move.

ACCUMULATED FORCE - The amassing of diverse sources of power which, when properly synchronized, produce an accumulative solitary force of proportionate effectiveness.

ACCUMULATIVE JOURNAL - An extensive notebook comprised of information on history, basics, descriptions of self-defense techniques as well as forms, terminology, anatomy, pledges, etc. The contents are authored by Ed Parker and are extremely helpful to progress-minded students who are anxious to sophisticate their knowledge of Kenpo.

ACTIVE CHI OR KI - The harmonious unification of the conscious and subconscious minds, synchronized with physical movement and proper breathing, to achieve overpowering feats. This method of achieving power is predominant among athletes, actors, dancers, and singers.

ACTOR - Tournament slang for one who fakes injury during freestyle or sparring competition.

ADD - The inclusion of a move prior to or after a base move has been executed; or the inclusion of one or more moves inserted intermittently or sporadically throughout a technique sequence. See PRE-FIX, SUFFIX, HIDDEN MOVES, INSERT, COMPOUNDING A TECHNIQUE and other related terms.

ADJUST - (1) The ability to alter, modify, adapt, or tailor our torso and limbs to a more suitable, operative, effective, and relevant position. (2) In the FORMULATION phase of Kenpo, adjust is a by-product of altering, whereby you can adjust the range (which affects depth), adjust the angle of execution (which affects width and height), and adjust both angle of execution and range (simultaneously).

ADVANCE(D) - (1) To move forward toward an opponent. (2) Progressive development and improvement in the Martial Arts.

ADVANCED MOVES - Sophisticated moves that require greater skill to perform. They are much more technical and thought-provoking. It is a term that is often interchangeable with ACCELERATED MOVES.

AGGRESSIVE OFFENSE - (1) The activation of the first attacking move without your opponent being aware of it. (2) An example of one of the three definitions that can be applied when executing an upward block.

 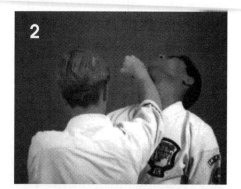

AGGRESSOR - One who initiates an unprovoked attack.

AGILITY - The development of sufficient flexibility, coordination and strength, such that when executing defensive and offensive movements, they may be performed skillfully and easily.

AIKIDO - A sophisticated form of Jiu-Jitsu employing circular movements to disrupt an opponent's balance by continuously redirecting the force of the aggressor. Included in the movements are throws, locks, twists, and strikes to joints and pressure points.

AIMING - (1) The pointing of a weapon (natural or man-made) so that it will follow a direct course of action when propelled toward the selected target. Depending on the intended target and the weapon to be used, other parts of the body may be selected as guides in giving proper aim when executing a chosen weapon. As an example, the knee may be directed to an opponent's chin just prior to your executing a front thrust ball kick. The knee, in this case, when properly aligned, can insure the accuracy of the front thrust ball kick. (2) Use of CONTOURING to help improve your accuracy. See CONTOUR GUIDANCE.

AIRBORNE - To move, using air space, to either escape or attack an opponent. This can be done by leaping, jumping, or diving.

AIRBORNE TECHNIQUES - Techniques delivered while in the air. Such moves are activated after a leap or jump in the air has been initiated.

ALIGNMENT - The precise adjustment of our torso and limbs so that they are arranged in direct line with each other for the purpose of utilizing total body mass. Refer to BODY ALIGNMENT and BACK-UP MASS for additional clarification.

ALPHABET OF MOTION - Each move learned, whether used defensively, offensively, or for both purposes, constitutes a letter in the ALPHABET OF MOTION.

ALTER - To vary a weapon and/or target within a technique sequence.

AMBIDEXTROUS - The ability to perform with equal agility on either side of the body (right or left).

AMERICAN KENPO - (1) An updated and all-inclusive version of Kenpo, based on logic and practicality, that has been designed to cope with the mode of fighting prevalent on our streets today. (2) A term commandeered by, and credited to Ed Parker.

AMPLIFICATION - Conversion of a move in a technique sequence from an offensive to a defensive application, or vice versa, without disrupting the continuous flow of action.

ANALOGY OF APPENDIX/DICTIONARY/ENCYCLOPEDIA - This analogy is used to distinguish and explain Kenpo forms and sets. Kenpo practitioners are instructed that all forms up to Short Form Three (Long and Short Forms One and Two) are comparable to the dictionary, whereby movements in the form can be defined. Short Form Three and above are compared to an encyclopedia. In these forms the movements are not only defined, but explained as well. Sets (Coordination, Stance, Blocking, Finger, Kicking, etc.) are considered appendices in that they are supplementary catalogues of motion that add to the general knowledge of a Kenpo student.

ANALOGY OF BUMPER/TRUCK - To some, FOCUS is when all sources of power have been conveyed to the weapon itself so that when contact is made it is only the weapon, like a projectile, and the target that are in FOCUS with each other. In Kenpo, however, FOCUS is the concentration of mind, body, breath and strength culminating at the exact instant when blocking or striking a specific target. It isn't just the mass of the natural weapon as it strikes the target, but rather the entire mass of the body synchronized with, and enhancing that natural weapon, that maximizes power. Stated simply, the entire body, not just the weapon, must be in FOCUS with the target to fully utilize mass. The mass of the natural weapon does start off independent of body mass, but developing velocity, it culminates upon impact with the other elements. Mass takes in the entire body, and not just a portion of it. Using a ten ton truck as an analogy, it is not the bumper of the truck that is in FOCUS with the wall when striking it at forty miles an hour, but the entire mass of the truck. ▼

(1) It is not the arm (bumper) alone that causes an effective strike, (2) but the back up mass of the body (Truck) as well as the arm.

ANALOGY OF FAST LUNCH/WEEK-END DINNER - This analogy explains the procedure used in jamming the depth zones of your opponent. It teaches you to first strike the targets closest to you, and then proceed toward the major targets of your opponent. These strikes not only injure, they become automatic checks which keep your opponent from retaliating. As your strikes work their way toward your opponent they are compared to having (1) a simple lunch where you eat a sandwich and drink a coke, (2) or to the rituals of a week-end dinner. If you were overly anxious to strike a major target such as your opponent's face, stomach, or ribs you would be guilty of trying to immediately go for a main dish. This type of strategy usually entails your going over, under, or around an opponent's defense to get to your main target or dish. This can be dangerous since your opponent can strike you on your way in, and get a sandwich out of you, so to speak. Striking and jamming the closest targets, and then proceeding to the furthest targets from you can be compared to the procedures followed when having a week-end

(1) Appetizer/coke (finger break, etc.), (2) salad/sandwich (Instep and/or knee break), (3) vegetables (elbow sprain or break), (4) rice pilaf (nose or eye rupture), (5) steak & lobster (rib break & testicle rupture, (6) desert (buckle), (7) after dinner mint (check please).

dinner. The first strike and jam could be paralleled to a cocktail, the second to a salad, the third to a bowl of soup, the fourth to the main dish, and the fifth to dessert as you cover out.

ANALOGY OF JET AIRCRAFT/AIRCRAFT CARRIER - This analogy parallels the principles involved in LAUNCHING a jet aircraft from the deck of an aircraft carrier and those involved in the execution of a punch. The fist is compared to an aircraft, and the legs to a catapult. When harmoniously employed, the two forces (punch and leg shuffle) not only maximize power, they allow the opposite hand to act as a check. Use of this principle triggers the BLACK-DOT-FOCUS concept. See PLANE THEORY and CATAPULT(ING).

thrusting arm

Catapulting leg

ANALOGY OF NOTES IN MUSIC - A comparative study of music and the Martial Arts will show that both are founded on basics. In music, the audible note is the underlying basic, while in the martial arts it is the physical move that plays that elemental role. In order to distinguish one note from another in music, notes are placed on a staff consisting of five parallel lines and the spaces between them. When these notes are written on the lines and in the spaces, they represent sounds or pitches that are identified by using the first seven letters of the alphabet. After the seventh note, they are repeated over

again in regular succession, starting with the first note. The moves in the Martial Arts are similarly distinguishable. When the upper limbs are employed, those moves are labeled as blocks, punches, chops, strikes, pokes, etc. If the lower limbs are employed, their moves are called kicks and stomps. While notes vary in pitch ranging from low to high, depending on the desired musical effect, likewise, lower targets call for movements utilizing the leg weapons; higher targets normally require moves utilizing the arms. In principle, then, we can say that we have low pitch weapons (moves) and high pitch weapons (moves), as music has high and low pitch notes. Further, notes can be altered by sharps and flats. A sharp raises a note one-half step, while a flat lowers a note one-half step. A similar comparison could be made when altering the type of natural weapon employed. If a knife-edged chop (sharp portion of the hand) was used as a weapon, it would raise or increase the amount of damage to a target, while the back of the hand (flat portion of the hand) would lower, or decrease the amount of damage.

ANALOGY OF PRINT/SCRIPT/SHORTHAND - This analogy best explains the types of movements that exist when practicing the martial arts. Here, students are made to see how motion can be compared to the three methods used when writing our language: print, script (cursive), and shorthand.

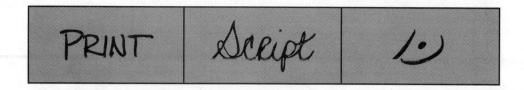

Printing employs circles, as well as curved and straight lines which parallel, and/or join each other at various points, but always break away to form individual letters. Such writing requires stopping one action before starting another. This stopping and starting action utilizes movements that lose time. Printed motion is predominant among Japanese and Korean stylists. Script (cursive), on the other hand, flows from one letter to the next, taking less time to write. This is true because script combines the straight and circular lines of the individual letters and then connects them on a continuous line that breaks only when an entire word is completed. Even though the lines in script often retrace their paths, one stroke does not have to stop before another begins. The flow is continuous, and the speed enhanced. Motion related to script can be found most often among Chinese and Kenpo stylists. In shorthand you have combinations of printing and script writing. These symbolic characters have been condensed in length and space, and their meaning increased. A few pen strokes or simple characters may have lengthy meanings. Likewise, in the Art, one punch may have two or more effects. It may change an offense to a defense, and then back to an offense again, or vice versa. Kenpo stylists, in addition to favoring motions related to script, enjoy employing shorthand motion.

ANALOGY OF SOLID/LIQUID/GAS - This analogy is used to help students understand motion from a different perspective. It compares motion with the three states of water (H_2O) — solid (ice), liquid, and gas (steam). Movements that are rigid and powerful can be compared to ice. They are solid in their execution. Those moves that flow like script writing can be compared to liquid, which not only flows, but seeks its own level. Moves that are simultaneously executed in several directions can be compared to the gaseous state of H_2O. Water in its gaseous state seeks its volume. Likewise, moves that simultaneously seek their range in several directions can be considered to be the gaseous state of motion.

ANALOGY OF SQUEEGEE - This analogy teaches you to parallel your moves with that of a squeegee. This principle allows you to simultaneously use upper and lower case movements, while retracing a path of motion. Retracing a path of motion affords you greater margin for error; therefore, it is much more logical to employ in terms of safety. Refer to SQUEEGEE PRINCIPLE.

ANALOGY OF TEA KETTLE - This analogy asks you to parallel your breathing with the process in a tea kettle, where heated water is converted to steam, and then forced to travel through a small opening or spout. The result is a more intense and better focused release of energy. This principle teaches that when steam or air is condensed, the force is greater. In a similar manner, condensed breathing, like condensed steam under pressure, proportionately increases the force rendered. Refer to TEA KETTLE PRINCIPLE.

ANATOMICAL POSITIONING - The calculated striking, forcing, or controlling of vital targets which will force an opponent into preconceived postural positions, and make the next anticipated target readily accessible for a follow-up.

ANATOMICAL WEAK POINTS - Essential body parts such as: the (1) temple, (2) throat, (3) mastoid, cervical spine, (4) solar plexus, kidney, (5) heart, (6) groin, (7) knee and others, which when struck can render an opponent helpless, or affect him fatally. See TARGETS and VITAL AREAS.

ANATOMY - The study of the human body structure, which aids in determining the vital striking areas on an opponent, as well as determining those body parts which could be readily used as natural weapons or defenses.

ANCHOR - To weigh down the elbow or buttocks for better leverage, coverage, or control. For example, the elbow is firmly fixed at a much lower level than the fist when executing an inward block. This principle, when applied, gives better bracing angle, more force, and allows a greater margin for error, in that it gives one greater protection.

AND - A word in the Kenpo vocabulary that causes one to employ one or more wasted beats (counts). This practice is eliminated by the more adept, as it involves wasted time and, therefore, is contradictory to ECONOMY OF MOTION. In Kenpo one does not allow the word "and" between strikes, but the word "with". As one strike is delivered, it is coupled "with" another. The term "with" does not imply an extra beat, as does the term "and".

ANGLE - (1) A specific degree of approach which one follows when delivering a weapon (natural or man-made) to a target. A specific viewpoint from which you or your opponent can be observed. (2) The direction and degree needed in having the surfaces of two planes (natural or man-made weapon, and target) meet.

ANGLE ALIGNMENT - The ability to adjust the path of your impending strike into proper perspective and approach. ▼

ANGLE(S) OF ATTACK - The eight major directions from which you or an opponent can attack or defend.

ANGLE OF CANCELLATION - A controlled angle which places an opponent in a precarious position, thus minimizing or even nullifying the use of his weapons. Prior to control, the angle could be created by directly meeting the

Cancelled width

Cancelled hight & width

Cancelled hight, width & depth

force, employing total collision, or triggered by a partial angle of deflection by either meeting or riding the force.

ANGLE OF CONTACT - Any angle which when delivering an offense or defense, produces the most desired effect. In some cases, a delivery may produce a dual effect. Exact or true right angle contact is not necessarily involved in the execution of these types of moves. ▼

ANGLE OF DEFLECTION - (1) That increased angle caused by a block, parry or otherwise, which widely gaps the weapon from the target. (2) The concept that the sooner you meet point "X" (the point of contact) the greater point ▼

"Y" (the distance of your opponent's weapon from you) will be. The concept is "to beat action, meet it." It is always best to meet your opponent's attacking weapon at a distance from you. The further the point of contact (point "X") is from you, the greater the miss (point "Y") will be from your face or body.

ANGLE OF DELIVERY - The position from which one's natural weapons may be executed with accuracy, efficiency, and effectiveness.

▶

ANGLE OF DEPARTURE - The most desired angle of escape when fading back or covering out and away from an opponent.

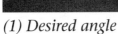

(1) Desired angle   *(2) Departs to zone of sanctuary*

ANGLE OF DESIRED POSITIONING - Another phrase to best describe ANGLE OF EFFICIENCY.

ANGLE OF DEVIATION - Securing the most desired angle when getting out of the line of attack, but allowing that same angle to enhance your own angle of attack or execution.

ANGLE OF DISTURBANCE - That angle which, when a move is executed, does not necessarily injure, but rather upsets an opponent's balance.

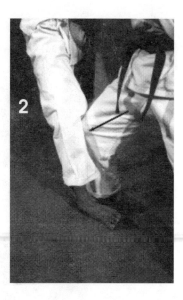

ANGLE OF EFFICIENCY - Refers to (1) the positioning of your feet and/or body whereby the alternatives in terms of weapon availability are increased proportionately; (2) The positioning of one's body to make a particular attack more operative or effective. ▼

Impact adjustment

ANGLE OF ENTRY - Any degree, or path (angle) of approach, whether linear or circular in execution, that allows you or your opponent access to specific targets. The path of approach can be executed horizontally, diagonally or vertically from any direction.

ANGLE OF ENTRY VS. LINE OF ENTRY - ANGLE OF ENTRY is any degree, or path (angle) of approach, whether linear or circular in execution, that allows you or your opponent access to specific targets. The path of approach can be executed horizontally, diagonally or vertically from any direction. LINE OF

ENTRY demands a specific path and direction of entry. It is that line or path of penetration that allows you or your opponent access to targets via vertical ascension or descension. The weapon may be executed vertically upward or downward depending on whether you or your opponent are standing or in a prone position. To thwart your opponent's efforts you may (depending on your lead leg and how it is matched with that of your opponent's lead leg) be (1) on the line of entry, (2) on top of the line of entry (on top of your opponent's foot), (3) inside of the line of entry, or (4) over the line of entry.

ANGLE OF EXECUTION - Any angle which, when an attack is executed, produces maximum results. Refer to ANGLE OF CONTACT.

ANGLE OF GREATEST MOVEMENT - That body position which enables one to move rapidly, easily, and without hesitation.

ANGLE OF INCIDENCE - The angle at which a weapon, when delivered, strikes perpendicular or at a right angle to the target or surface intended, to bring about maximum results.

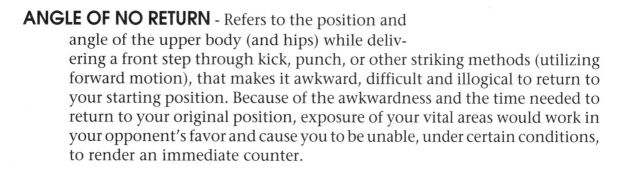

ANGLE MATCHING - A non-contact method of CONTOURING employing the principle of COMPLIMENTARY ANGLE, MIRROR, SILHOUETTING, or REVERSE MIRROR IMAGE. See SYMMETRICAL. See MATCHING COUNTER.

ANGLE OF MOBILITY - Any degree, or path of approach void of encumbrances.

ANGLE OF NO RETURN - Refers to the position and angle of the upper body (and hips) while delivering a front step through kick, punch, or other striking methods (utilizing forward motion), that makes it awkward, difficult and illogical to return to your starting position. Because of the awkwardness and the time needed to return to your original position, exposure of your vital areas would work in your opponent's favor and cause you to be unable, under certain conditions, to render an immediate counter.

ANGLE OF RETURN - The position and angle of the upper body (and hips) while delivering a kick or punch at which it is feasible for you to return to your original or starting position without difficulty.

ANGLE OF OBSCURITY - Achieving the proper angle so as to conceal the weapon you plan to use. A prime example can be found when employing the DEAD MOTION PRINCIPLE, where one arm is hidden by another to give the illusion that nothing is happening until it does happen.

ANGLE OF OPPORTUNITY - An angle which, when taking advantage of any and all of the "angle" classifications, results in the success of the effects desired and/or intended.

ANGLE OF PROTECTION - The positioning of your body to give you maximum shield against anticipated strikes.

ANGLING THE GAP - Abstaining from approaching on a straight line when bridging the distance between you and your opponent. Angles other than a straight, head-on approach are used instead.

ANGULAR ATTACK - Any attack void of a straight, head-on approach, and that exclude frontal attacks that are horizontal in nature.

ANGULAR AVOIDANCE - Awareness of the many angles of attack, other than a straight, head-on, frontal attack; this knowledge allows you the opportunity to withdraw or prevent attacks that may stem from such angles.

ANGULAR STRATEGY - The ability to devise or employ specific attacks from any angle, other than a straight line, so that an encounter with your opponent leaves you with advantageous conditions.

ANGULAR VERSATILITY - The available number of angles from which a weapon, natural or otherwise, can be effective at close range. The usefulness of any weapon, natural or otherwise, rests with the number of angles from which it can be effectively used, and it's distance from the target. An excellent example is the effective use of a knife at close range compared to the use of a gun. To grab a knife at close range would be illogical, since it could cut in any direction from which you might attempt to grab it. Given a close proximity, you would have a better chance to control a gun. This is

true because you could more safely grab the gun, and keep the line of fire away from you at all times. Its not the gun, but the bullet that you should be concerned with.

ANTICIPATE - To monitor action in advance, which results in predicting your opponent's intended moves.

ANTICIPATED VARIABLES - The ability to envision, contemplate, foresee, and activate instant solutions to altered predicaments.

APEX - Highest (uppermost) point of any circle or line. Again, depending upon your point of view, it could be the furthest point of the circle.

APEX OF A CIRCLE - Same as APEX.

APPRENTICE BLACK BELT - One who is recommended and permitted by his instructor to wear a Black Belt, but who is not officially certified until judged and passed by a Black Belt Board of Examiners.

AREA CHECK - To position body limbs (see POSITIONAL CHECK) so that they are readily available to cover and protect fairly wide areas of the body.

ARROW - A term used by the Chinese in describing stances, parts of which resemble an arrow.

ARTICULATION OF MOTION - (1) The combination of individual basics into a sequential flow of uninterrupted motion whereby each basic move remains crisp in its application. (2) The extemporaneous use of basic combinations where, regardless of number, each move is delivered with clarity and precision.

ARTICULATION OF MOTION VS. PHONETICS OF MOTION - Articulation of Motion entails the precise, specific, and distinct application of motion regardless of the speed employed. Each move, whether used separately or in a sequence of moves, is clear and well defined when executed. Phonetics of Motion involves detailing motion by-the-numbers. Specific moves are broken down into their component parts, whereby one learns to articulate or enunciate each move a segment at a time.

ASSOCIATED MOVES - Moves that are identical in principle, but multiple in definition. The term, to some degree, is related to FAMILY GROUPINGS and FAMILY RELATED MOVES.

ASSOCIATION PATCH - The Ed Parker's American Kenpo logo placed over the heart on the left side of the gi(uniform). This patch was concievied and designed by Ed Parker in the late 1950's and illustrated by his brother David P. Parker. See Kenpo Crest.

ATTENTION - (1) The erect, motionless posture of students in readiness for another command. (2) A command to assume this posture.

ATTITUDE - (1) Pertains to an individual's mental disposition, traits of which can be positive or negative. (2) The postural structure of your body when in combat that displays the feeling or mood you are in. Depending upon your disposition, your body language can intimidate or invite aggression.

AVAILABLE - State of being ready for immediate action.

AVAILABILITY OF TARGETS - Target areas that are conveniently accessible.

AVAILABILITY OF WEAPONS - Readiness of weapons (natural or man-made) for immediate use to target areas that are accessible.

AXIS OF ROTATION - See ROTATING AXIS.

B

BACKING - Use of body parts as a support or brace when striking a target. This support allows the principle of SANDWICHING to occur. For example, one arm braces as the other strikes. ▶

BACKSTOP - A support or brace for a target that is being SANDWICHED. ▶

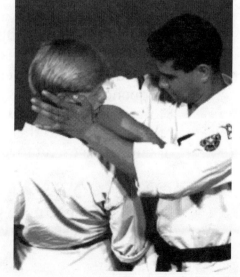

BACK-UP-MASS - The use of body weight that is directly behind the action that is taking place. As example, (1) a punch delivered when the elbow is directly behind the fist, or (2) the bracing of one finger directly behind the other when delivering a two finger chop to the throat, etc. BACK-UP-MASS is greatly enhanced when proper BODY ALIGNMENT is achieved. BODY ALIGNMENT gets MASS into proper perspective and allows the body to take full advantage of channeling weight and energy while traveling in the same direction (DIRECTIONAL HARMONY).

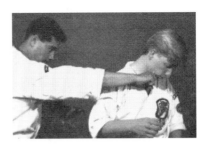

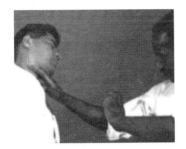

BACK-UP WEAPON - A secondary weapon that is available and ready to use.

BALANCE - Stability produced by distributing your weight proportionately, regardless of body posture. In short, it is the body poised harmoniously.

BALANCE COMPENSATION - The continuous adjustment of your balance each time defensive or offensive contact is made with an opponent.

BANGER - An individual who has no control. (Tournament slang.)

BASE LINE(S) - Imaginary line or lines used to visualize the angle on which you are to concentrate your attention. See LINE OF SIGHT.

BASE MOVE - Any move you decide to use as a POINT OF REFERENCE.

BASICS - Simplified moves that comprise the fundamentals of Kenpo. They are divided into stances, maneuvers, blocks, strikes, punches, kicks, finger techniques, parries, specialized moves and methods.

BEFORE - A move that is added prior to your BASE MOVE. It is the move that you choose as your prefix, in order to complete the EQUATION FORMULA.

BEGGING HANDS - A term given to one of the self-defense techniques (Blue Belt Technique #1) describing the position of the hands during the execution of the technique. The hands are positioned as if begging for money.

BELT RANKING SYSTEM - A colored belt system used to grade a student's ability and proficiency. Such judgment is determined after a student undergoes a performance test. The sequence of the colors is; white, yellow, orange, purple, blue, green, 3rd., 2nd., and 1st degree brown, and ten degrees of black, tenth being the highest.

BIND - To tie up, or to prevent one from retaliating. This is another method of CHECKING. ▼

BITING - A specialized vice-like method using the teeth to injure an opponent. It is especially useful when both hands and feet are inoperable.

BLACK BELT DEGREES - First degree is Junior Instructor; second degree is Associate Instructor; third degree is Head Instructor; fourth degree is Senior Instructor; fifth degree is Associate Professor; sixth degree is Professor; seventh degree is Senior Professor; eighth degree is Associate Master of the Arts; ninth degree is Master of the Arts; and tenth degree is Grand Master of the Arts. The tenth degree founder and head of the system is known as the Senior Grand Master of the Arts. Only upon the founder of the system may this title be bestowed. ▼

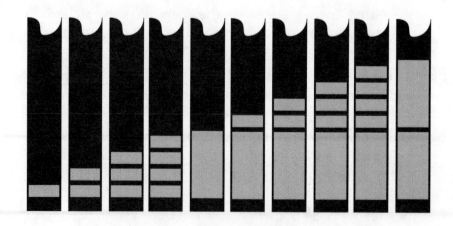

BLACK DOT FOCUS - Our Kenpo concept of focus. We visualize a black dot on a white background, representing total awareness. Our concern is not only with maximizing power, but protection as well. See WHITE DOT FOCUS.

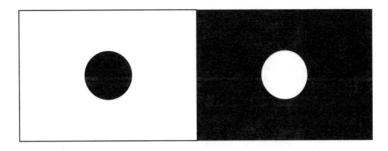

BLIND SPOT(S) - Areas that are not obvious to the eye. Obscure areas that lie outside the boundaries of peripheral sight. See OBSCURE ZONES.

BLOCKADE - The employment of a barrier to obstruct the efforts of an attacking opponent.

BLOCK(S) - A defensive maneuver used to hinder or check an attack; all defensive moves employing physical contact to check, cushion, deflect, redirect, or stop an offensive move.

BOB AND WEAVE - Body maneuvers used to avoid an attack. A BOB employs vertical movements of the body. A WEAVE utilizes horizontal, side to side, movements of the body.

BOBBING - A method of avoiding an attack while vertically dropping underneath, or rising above the action of your opponent. DUCKING is a stage of BOBBING.

BODY ALIGNMENT - This is the coordination of body parts in order to harmonize their angles of travel so that they all move together, in line, and in one direction. This principle, when followed, automatically triggers the principle of BACK-UP-MASS, where body weight enhances your action.

BODY COMMUNICATION - The giving and receiving of information by body movements, mannerisms, expressions, gestures, habits, etc.

BODY FULCRUM - The natural curvatures of the body used as launching platforms to add leverage, bracing, or acceleration to the speed and force of any weapon. It is classified as a method of CONTOURING. Also refer to LEVER-AGING.

BODY FUSION - A concept in which body parts move as a unit prior to relaying action to other parts of the body. These body parts are literally fused together in order to function as a single unit. A good example is when the wrist and elbow joints are in a fixed position so that only the shoulder joint is allowed to move. Body fusion can occur any time during the course of a sequential flow of action.

BODY HARMONY - All body parts functioning as one unit.

BODY INTERPRETATION - The translation or reading of body movements, mannerisms, expressions, gestures, habits, etc., one uses in predetermining an opponent's true intentions.

BODY LANGUAGE - Communication with body movements, mannerisms, expressions, gestures, habits, etc. in relaying true or false information. Refer to BODY COMMUNICATION.

BODY MECHANICS - The technical utilization of the body in the science of motion and action, that allows the forces therein to be fully maximized. In short, highly technical knowledge of the proper use of the body in reaching or obtaining maximum results.

BODY MOMENTUM - Body weight used to increase the force of your action. It involves the coordination of mind, breath, strength, and body weight so that all forces are moving in harmony in the same direction (DIRECTIONAL HARMONY). There are three basic ways to obtain body momentum; (1) by shuffling forward or reverse on a horizontal plane, thus employing the dimension of depth; (2) by utilizing gravitational marriage on a vertical or diagonal plane, which fulfills the dimension of height; and (3) by torquing the body to create body rotation, thus completing the dimension of width. All three methods of acquiring body momentum can be applied singularly, in partial combination, or when combining all three methods of body momentum. It is a great contributor to BACK-UP-MASS which places body alignment in proper perspective.

BODY ROTATION - Body torque used to increase the force of your strike or action. It is a means of generating BODY MOMEMTUM via the dimension of WIDTH. It may also be used to form an in-place TWIST STANCE.

BODY TRANSLATION - The decoding of body movements that gives one answers to an opponent's true intentions. Refer to BODY INTERPRETATION.

BORROWED FORCE - An opponent's force which is used against him. This can be accomplished by going with the opponent's force, or on occasion, going against his force. The concept allows your opponent's force to enhance the effectiveness of your action.

BOUNCE(ING) - A method that is purposely used to cause an opponent's reaction, and makes your follow-up move easy to execute. For example, in the self-defense technique named LEAP OF DEATH, two heel palm strikes are used on the back of your

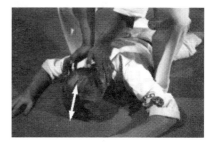

opponent's head (which is face down at the time). This action is instrumental in forcing your opponent's face to hit the ground with great impact, and thus causes an instinctive reaction, whereby your opponent will immediately lift his head off the ground. When this occurs, both of your hands are then free to slide under the chin of your opponent and continue further devastating action, such as wrenching or snapping his neck.

BOW - Involves the bending of your head and/or waist from an attention stance for a short period of time before raising back to your original position. Practitioners of American Kenpo are taught to bow only to inanimate objects. Whenever a student enters or leaves the training room he bows as a symbol of respect, not worship.

BRACING ANGLE - That specific body position which strengthens and supports the execution of a defensive or offensive move in anticipation of contact or impact. See IMPACT ADJUSTMENT.

BRANCH - A term referring to the leg when used in self-defense techniques.

BREAK - (1) Force, which when effectively employed, shatters, splinters, cracks, detaches, disjoins, or separates bones or their joints. (2) A term used to separate two contestants emotionally involved in a match.

BRIDGE - To close and link the gaps that occur between you and your opponent. See CLOSING THE GAP.

BROKEN RHYTHM - Erratically timed movements that follow no set beat or pattern, but which can be deliberately used to deceive or interrupt the action of an opponent. A simple analogy — the pre-meditated use of stuttering motion. This term is related to DECEPTIVE TIMING. (See DELAYED MOVEMENT, RETARDED MOVEMENT, and STUTTERING MOTION.)

BROTHER/SISTER MOVES - Moves evolving from FAMILY GROUPINGS. These moves are alternatives that can stem from your first initial action. See FAMILY GROUPINGS.

BUCKLE - Methods used to force an opponent's leg to bend in or out, forward or back. Properly used, it can unbalance, twist, sprain or even break an opponent's leg.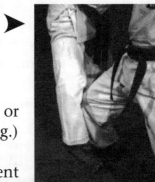

BUMMER - A bad call regarding receiving a point, penalty, or disqualification at a tournament. (Tournament slang.)

BUMPING - A specialized method used to push an opponent away from you.

BUOYANCY - The ability to rise or float to the surface. In Kenpo, moves are not executed when inhaling, but when exhaling. Exhaling settles your body, stabilizes your base, and greatly enhances the force of your delivery. On the other hand, inhaling makes one buoyant and unstable, especially when blocking or striking. Buoyancy, however, can be an asset when covering out. It seems that the body is lighter and much more free to move about when buoyant.

BUTTING - Specialized methods which utilize the head as a weapon. The head can be used to thrust, hook, or hammer with.

BY-THE-NUMBERS - Methods used to teach movements to beginning students where each step is given a number. This is similar to learning words by syllables and pronouncing them phonetically.

CAPOEIRA - An excellent Brazilian method of self-defense. Experts of Capoeira resemble graceful dancers. They employ cartwheels, handsprings, ground techniques, and takedowns to effectively subdue their opponents.

CATAPULT(ING) - Methods that are used to help launch or spring you forward with your action. For example, a "push drag shuffle" can be used to spring forward simultaneously with a punch. Thus, the launching (catapulting) of the lower half of the body, simultaneous with the execution of the punch, greatly enhances your power. CATAPULTING activates BODY MOMENTUM. Refer to PLANE THEORY.

CAT AROUND - This term refers to having a foot slide around and back of another person's leg, where the transition of such a move resembles a cat stance, prior to settling into its final position.

CATCH(ES) - A method of stopping and detaining an opponent's strike or block.

CAT STANCE - Usually a transitory stance with 90% of the body weight centered low, on the rear leg, and with the rear foot flat. The forward leg rests lightly on the ball of the foot, as if poised for a kick.

CENTER OF GRAVITY - That point around which one's weight is evenly distributed so that your body is kept in constant balance to help maximize your physical movements.

CENTER OF MASS - An odd phenomenon where maximum power can still be obtained though the center of mass remains stationary, and the body limbs strike out in opposite directions. This phenomenon can only work if the center of your body mass remains centered regardless of the opposing forces

of your limbs. Although it appears as if directional harmony is void during this type of action, power, nevertheless, is still enhanced. The opposing forces of the limbs are not assisted in anyway by the center of your body mass, which remains neutral. As already stated, it is an odd phenomenon, but experience affirms its reality. See MID-POINT BALANCE.

CENTRIFUGAL FORCE - A force that tends to make rotating bodies move away from the center of rotation.

CHAMBERING - The cocking of a natural weapon prior to striking with it.

CHAMBERED POSITION - The cocked position of a natural weapon that's ready for action. It is often referred to as CHAMBERING.

CHANGING OF THE GUARD - A phrase used to describe the continuous changing of hands or feet during combat to insure constant protection against intentional as well as unintentional attacks. The continuous relocation of body parts also helps in counterbalancing your movements.

CHARGER - An opponent who rushes straight in. (Tournament slang.)

CHEAT - (1) To execute a deceptive move prior to the one intended. This includes utilizing hands and/or feet. (2) To use an additional move, when doing a KATA or FORM, in order to place you in proper position or alignment.

CHECK - To restrain, hinder, or prevent an opponent from taking action. This is accomplished by pressing, pinning, or hugging an opponent, usually at the joints, so that it minimizes his leverage and nullifies his action. Positioning your arms and legs in various defensive postures can also keep an opponent from striking you effectively. See POSITIONAL CHECK.

CHECKING COCK - A defensive move used as a check, but which also remains in an appropriate pose so that it is readily available for an immediate attack or counter attack.

CHECKING VS. CONTROLLING - Checking involves momentary prevention; whereas, controlling entails prolonged deterrence.

CHI - A Chinese term used to describe the powers that can be generated when the mind and body are totally unified. It involves total and complete synchronization of mind, breath, and strength to achieve maximum force. It is that extra inner force created by the precise synchronization of the conscious and subconscious mind, along with an individual's breath and strength.

CHICKEN KICK - A double kick combination that starts with one leg kicking while the other supports the body weight. When the supporting leg is employed, as the second kick, both legs become air-borne during its execution. There are two basic methods of application: (1) kick first with the forward leg before employing the rear leg, or (2) commence with the rear leg before executing the forward leg.

CHINESE FAN PRINCIPLE - Principle that teaches how reaction can beat action by simply moving the target first, and not the blocking arm. This principle takes advantage of the time it takes for a weapon to reach its target. Since the target is the last contact point that an opponent must reach, moving it out of the way first, helps your reaction to beat your opponent's action.

CH'I SAO - A training method developed, practiced, and popularized by Wing Chun stylists. The term means STICKY HANDS. The concept involves the sensitive use of the arms, rather than the eyesight, to determine the release of a punch or strike.

CHOKING - Specialized vice-like methods used to cut off breathing.

CHOP - A cutting blow to an opponent or object, which generally employs the knife-edge of the hand as the weapon.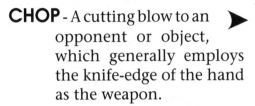

CHU'AN SHU - Is a term used in mainland China to describe the western term of Kung Fu.

CIRCULAR CONFINEMENT - The restriction of circular moves from following a wider path or orbit. Causes of restriction may stem from environment, or from parts of your opponent's (or your own) anatomy being in the way.

Restricted roundhouse punch   *Confined between wrist & face*

CIRCULAR MOVEMENTS - Moves that loop or follow a rounded path. Such moves can be used defensively or offensively, and can orbit in a single direction, or be diverted into multiple directions.

CIRCULAR ROTATION - Rotation of your arm in a circle to build momentum prior to the final torquing action of your strike.

CLASSICAL - A term used to describe the so called pure systems of Karate or Kung Fu. Many of the movements associated with these systems are not practical in our present environment, since their methods were created for the types of defense found prevalent during their particular time in history.

CLAWING - Striking action employing the fingertips to scratch or rip. Such action may employ two or more fingers.

CLEARING - (1) The diverting of strikes from making contact. (2) The moving of a defensive posture to create a target opening. (3) The sweeping of a path that will guarantee clear passage.

CLOCK PRINCIPLE - A method used to help students visualize the direction in which they are to move. Students are generally asked to think of themselves as being in the middle of a big clock facing 12 o'clock, with 6 o'clock to their rear, 3 and 9 to their right and left, and all other numbers in their respective locations.

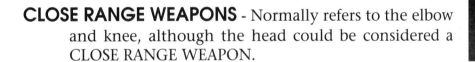

CLOSE KNEEL STANCE - Similar to a neutral bow stance, with the exception that the rear knee is dropped two inches from the ground. The rear knee is kept in as well as close to the forward leg. The weight of the body is equally divided on both legs. The WIDE and CLOSE KNEEL STANCES obtain their names because of the width, and not depth that exist between them.

CLOSE RANGE - See CLOSE RANGE ENCOUNTERS.

CLOSE RANGE ENCOUNTERS - Action that occurs within elbow and knee distance.

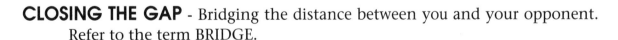

CLOSE RANGE WEAPONS - Normally refers to the elbow and knee, although the head could be considered a CLOSE RANGE WEAPON.

CLOSING THE GAP - Bridging the distance between you and your opponent. Refer to the term BRIDGE.

CLOSING THE GATE - Constricting your width and height zones by repositioning your stance, body, or arms so that vulnerability is kept to a minimum.

COCKING CHECK - The positioning of a check that remains in an appropriate pose so that it is readily available for an immediate attack or counter attack.

COLLAPSIBLE DEFLECTION - The strategic bending of a defensive move, in order to make it more functional as an additional defense. This can apply to your or your opponent's moves where the secondary action can readily be used to deflect a second attacking weapon. Collapsing the arm makes it functional in two ways: (1) it converts into a very effective defense before (2) returning it as a full length offense. Failing to collapse an opponent's arm can, however, be detrimental if it gets in the way of your action.

COLLAPSING CHECK - An existing check, which when dropped, gravitates into a secondary position of defense.

COLLIDING FORCES - The clashing of various sources of power that can work against you, or be tailored to work for you. While many feel that one should always go with the force, strategically planned opposition to force can often be very rewarding.

COMBAT - Realistic fighting which excludes control and rules.

COMBAT ARENA - Any area in which an encounter can occur. Again, environment dictates the type of arena that it might be.

COMBAT AWARENESS - In tune with what is or can be expected in a realistic fight.

COMBAT EFFECTIVENESS - Competent and productive use of your skills during a skirmish or an all out attack.

COMBO MAN - An individual who uses both hands and feet equally as well when scoring. He believes in using a series of techniques to gain points. (Tournament slang.)

COMMITTED ACTION - Movement which binds one to a certain line of action.

COMMON SENSE - (1) The use of sound and practical judgment; (2) the inherent ability to view things logically when overcoming difficult problems and situations. See HORSE SENSE.

COMPACT UNIT - The constriction of body parts to enhance the effectiveness of a strike. For example, the pinching together of the forearm and biceps, when striking with your elbow, makes for a more compact unit. Creating this formation allows your BACK-UP-MASS to produce an even greater amount of force upon impact.

COMPARISONS OF BASICS - Basics can be compared to a dictionary, encyclopedia, or appendix. A dictionary defines and is comparable to Forms, Short #1 through Long #2. An encyclopedia explains in greater detail, and could be compared to Short #3 through #9, as well as to self-defense techniques. An appendix gives additional information, and can be compared to all of the sets that are learned in Kenpo.

COMPARISONS OF MOTION - Motion can be compared to the three methods of writing — print, script (cursive), and shorthand; or the three stages of matter — solid, liquid, and gas (vapor).

COMPARATIVE ANALYSIS - The ability to examine other fields of endeavor, assess their similarities, and match them with your present topic of study so that your understanding can be increased proportionately.

COMPENSATE - To move in such a manner that ROOM FOR ERROR, or adjustment on the part of the deliverer, is allowed.

COMPLEMENTARY ANGLE - A strike or block that follows a path or angle that parallels an attacking weapon, a defensive posture, the contour of your or your opponent's body, or a given line. Following these angular paths allows clear entry to desired targets. Taking advantage of these angular opportunities helps to produce greater accuracy and damage, and thus maximizes results.

COMPLETE HARMONY - Mind, breath, and strength coordinated to function in total unison.

COMPLETED PATH OF TRAVEL - The termination of a move that may have followed a horizontal, vertical, or diagonal path. Should a combination of moves be used, the termination of each would be described as being Completed Paths of Travel.

COMPOUNDING A TECHNIQUE - The insertion of additional moves that are within the flow of a prescribed technique or selected sequence of action. More often than not, these inserted moves are simultaneously executed along with the base moves of a technique sequence. COMPOUNDING can occur during the IDEAL PHASE (normal flow), or the WHAT IF? PHASE (altered flow — change of target and definition) of a technique. It is possible to further COMPOUND your action while in the process of COMPOUND-ING. Unless these moves are displayed, they can very easily remain hidden.

COMPRESSING DISTANCE - Slowly, but surely, reducing the gap that exists between you and your opponent when contestants at a tournament or when involved in combat.

CONCAVE - Arched or curved in.

CONCAVE STANCE - A type of stance where the knees are curved in to insure protection. It may also be used as a support or brace to enhance the effectiveness of a counter. The self-defense technique LEAP OF DEATH graphically details the use of the CONCAVE STANCE.

CONCEALED CARRIES - Methods of positioning the Nunchaku on the body or clothing in order to gain easy access prior to an attack, and yet keep them hidden from view. See "Ed Parker's Guide to the Nunchaku".

CONCENTRATION - The focusing of one's attention (mental), or force (physical). Either (mental or physical) can be applied separately or in combination with each other.

CONCEPT - An abstract idea, conceived in the mind, that is neither protected nor trademarked.

CONCEPTUAL BOX - A visualization concept used to teach students how to obtain proper angles of execution. The concept entails visualizing the outline of a box in front of you. This imaginary box is then used as a guide to better understand the various paths and zones in which an arm or leg should travel when blocking or striking.

CONCHAKU - Newly innovated nunchaku made of polyresin developed by Francisco Conde.

CONDITIONED RESPONSE - An ingrained response to a given variable.

CONFLUENCE OF FORCES - The union of various sources of power, combinations of which can stem from you, or from both you and your opponent.

CONCRETE FACIAL - A slang term describing aggressive techniques that involve smashing your opponent's face to the concrete floor.

CONSCIOUS - (1) Alert and aware of your surroundings. (2) Having feeling and knowledge of what you are doing, and why.

CONSCIOUS MIND - The cognitive portion of our mind (brain) that allows us the ability to think while we are in an awakened, attentive state.

CONSTIPATED MOVES - Moves that tense prematurely, resulting in needless exertion that hinders speed. Describes those individuals who are so tense when blocking or striking that the speed and effect of their actions are hampered to a point of frustration.

CONSTITUENTS - Elements, parts, or components that add to the whole or sum total of an organization, society, system, or art such as Kenpo.

CONTACT - The joining together of target and weapon. The colliding of fist and face, foot and groin, elbow and jaw, etc.

CONTACT DEVIATION - The employment of any defensive move, which when contact is made, deflects the action of your opponent.

CONTACT MANIPULATION - The fourth stage of the FOUR STAGES OF RANGE. It entails the orchestration of control, once contact is made, to contour, leverage, takedown, restrain, twist, sprain, lock, dislocate, choke, etc. to increase the effectiveness of your action. These same techniques could be used to cause greater damage or injury to you as well, therefore, making every effort to be the victor.

CONTACT PENETRATION - The third stage of the FOUR STAGES OF RANGE. It refers to the distance in which a weapon can effectively penetrate the depths of a target, thus magnifying the damage or injury that can occur to you or your opponent.

CONTACT PLACEMENTS - A predetermination of the targets which you plan to strike, force, or control using the weapon or methods of your choice.

CONTINENTAL FORM - Slang for a form that is long in duration.

CONTINUITY - The principle that no move passes from one position to another without being utilized effectively. It is a counterpart of ECONOMY OF MOTION.

CONTINUOUS WEAPONS - A series of multiple natural weapons employed when involved in combat or freestyle.

CONTOUR CONFINEMENT - Keeping your movements within close proximity of your or your opponent's body so that the effects of your action become more acute. See ZONE CONFINEMENT.

CONTOUR DISCIPLINING - The enforcing of behavioral patterns to continuously keep your movements within close proximity of your or your opponent's body. See CONTOURING and ZONE DISCIPLINING.

CONTOUR GUIDANCE - Use of the contour of your or your opponent's body as a homing device or guide to improve the accuracy of your action. See AIMING.

CONTOURING - This concept involves using the outline of your or your opponent's body as a homing device or guide to accomplish certain feats. The concept is divided into two basic categories — methods that employ (1) body contact, or (2) non-body contact. Under body contact you have LAUNCHING, where the surface of your or your opponent's body is used to ricochet or bounce off of prior to traveling to your primary target. Another method employing body contact is LEVERAGING, where an opponent's body is used as a fulcrum to enhance your action. A SLIDING CHECK employs constant body contact as it moves from one leverage point to another. The FRICTIONAL PULL is another form of body contact that can be employed. Although it is used differently, it resembles a SLIDING CHECK. TRACKING or GUIDELINING involves sliding along the CONTOUR of your or your opponent's body which acts as a guide to your target. While both terms could be used interchangeably, TRACKING (which follows a line of action) requires specific methods to insure precisioned accuracy, where a natural weapon rides, tracks, and inches its way to the target (as in the technique DANCE OF DARKNESS where one hand inches its way up on the arm that remains at its target). GUIDELINING requires that a natural weapon follow a wider surface area (path of action), when guided to its target (as in the technique DANCE OF DEATH where the striking arm follows the entire surface of the hip and thigh on its way to the groin). THREADING is another body contact means of CONTOURING where the joint of your body is used to guide the natural weapon of your choice to its target. This can only occur if the two body parts that form the joint meet each other at specific angles so as to warrant its use. Unlike TRACKING, where the natural weapon inches its way from one spot to another as it travels to the target, THREADING requires that the natural weapon remain on one spot as it THREADS its way to the target. NEEDLING occurs when two natural weapons simultaneously TRACK their way to their targets. PIVOTING uses the body as an axis. Example — A heel palm strike to the chin can very easily be converted into a five finger slice by using the chin as the pivoting axis, thus using the principle of a WINDSHIELD WIPER. FITTING involves striking with specific NATURAL WEAPONS that form a perfect fit with the target being struck. This is also referred to as the PUZZLE PRINCIPLE. Other contact methods come in the form of GRAVITATIONAL CHECKS and PRESSING CHECKS that use the contour of the body to cause the effect desired. Non-body contact methods can be found under the topics of COMPLEMENTARY ANGLE, ANGLE MATCHING, SILHOUETTING, FRAMING, SYMMETRICAL, and CORRESPONDING ANGLES.

CONTROL - 1. The regulation of force to produce (a) accuracy as well as (b) the degree of injury. For example, a punch that strikes a specific target without injuring it requires control. Control may or may not involve touching your target. It takes even greater CONTROL to avoid injuring a person who is constantly moving.

2. The ability (a) to prevent or curtail your opponent's actions, or (b) to guide your opponent wherever, however, and whenever. Checks are types of controls. They are good examples of how one can temporarily prevent or curtail an opponent from taking action.

CONTROL ASSISTANCE - The use of additional body parts to assist you in securing control of your opponent.

CONTROLLING - (1) The ability to restrain oneself from all out action, or execute action with regulatory frequency and persistence. (2) The use of various techniques employed to restrain your opponent from taking all out action.

CONTROL MANIPULATION - To sustain control of your opponent's actions while steering or maneuvering your opponent to more suitable and strategic positions. Setting up these positions not only helps to prevent further retaliation, but allows you clear access to your opponent's targets as well.

CONTROL MAINTENANCE - To sustain control during the course of an encounter by continuing a particular grab, hold, lock, etc. Such action of stationary dominance deters further retaliation.

CONTROL RELEASE - The ability to set your opponent free after employing control maintenance and control manipulation whereby such freedom continues to disallow an opponent from further retaliation.

CONTROLLED RESPONSE - The regulation of one's actions so that he does not react prematurely, unnecessarily, or foolishly. This is especially true if an opponent should employ DECEPTIVE ACTION.

CONTROLLING THE GAP - The ability to control your distance once you have bridged or closed the gap (distance) between you and your opponent.

CONVERGING FORCES - Generally refers to both you and your opponent's forces clashing at some point. However, both forces can stem from you, such as you find when sandwiching. See COLLIDING FORCES.

COORDINATION - Refers to (1) the synchronization of all body parts so that they function with continuity, timing, and dexterity, (2) the synchronization of your moves with the moves, timing, and direction of your opponent in order to take best advantage of them and attack him more effectively.

COORDINATION SET I - Requirement for Purple Belt. It contains, basic blocks, stances, punches, kicks, and moves that are singular in motion, but dual in purpose.

COORDINATION SET II - Requirement for Green Belt.

CORKSCREW PUNCH - A torquing, twisting punch that strikes with the palm down.

CORRECTIVE ADJUSTMENT - A more appropriate term for constructive criticism.

CORRELATION OF FORCES - Various power sources simultaneously meeting at a point where directional harmony becomes the catalyst, synchronizing all power sources into one focused unit. It is this precise orchestration of power sources that greatly maximizes the effectiveness at the point of impact.

CORRESPONDING ANGLES - Matching the angles of your or your opponent's body parts and limbs, in order to maintain balance and symmetry. This term also falls under the heading of CONTOURING.

COUNTER(ING) - The ability to attack during or immediately after an opponent's attack.

COUNTERACTING FLOW - The execution of a move, or moves, that hinder maximizing your efforts. As an example; never use a right inward block while simultaneously executing a right forward bow, as one action diminishes the effectiveness of the other.

COUNTER BALANCE - (1) Opposing forces which enhance the effectiveness of a particular blow, maneuver or movement. (2) The continuous relocation of body parts in order to equalize your body weight in motion, as well as give you better protection. See CHANGING OF THE GUARD and BALANCE COMPENSATION.

COUNTER GUIDANCE - Allowing your opponent's action to guide you to targets on his body. For example, if an opponent's punch was caught by you, and he attempted to retrieve it, you could then go with his action, borrow his force, and "guide" his fist into his own face as a part of your "counter" action.

COUNTER MAN - Tournament slang for one who waits for his opponent to press the action before countering.

COUNTER MANIPULATION - (1) That stage of motion that is utilized just prior to employing the principle of opposing forces to its maximum. (2) The control of one body part to strike or manipulate another body part (same arm or another) to increase the effectiveness of your strike.

COUNTER PREVENTION - The ability to anticipate, meet, and stall an opponent's action in advance. See PREVENTIVE MOTION.

COUNTER ROTATION - (1) To reverse the action and path of your torque. (2) Turning or twirling in the opposite direction from the previous twirling move.

COVER - The repositioning of your body into a protective pose while creating distance between you and your opponent. This is usually done by shifting the forward leg to the opposite side as you turn and face the opposite direction. This maneuver will not only create distance, as you turn and face the unknown, but will help decelerate your opponent's action as well. A notable characteristic using this maneuver, when used as an exercise, and depending on the lead leg, is that you will continue to move laterally, away from your original stance.

COVER OUT - A single crossover and step through reverse to increase the distance between you and your opponent, thus enabling you to conclude your maneuver in a safe position of cover.

COVER STEP - The first step of a FRONT CROSSOVER (foot maneuver), which aids in concealing the groin area.

CRAB-HAND PINCH - A special method of forming and applying your hand to pinch with. The formation and use of the hand is like the pinchers found on a crab. An example of this is in the self-defense technique called *Grasp of Death*.

CREED - A modern code of ethics authored by Ed Parker for Martial Artists in today's environment. It reads as follows: *"I come to you with only Karate, empty hands. I have no weapons, but should I be forced to defend myself, my principles or my honor, should it be a matter of life or death, of right or wrong; then here are my weapons, Karate, my empty hands."*

CREED VS. PLEDGE - The CREED has become an accepted Code for many Martial Artists. It denotes the Martial Artist's way of life in today's environment. Equally as important, the Creed acts as a guide to the Martial Artist in developing a keen sense of justice. The PLEDGES are extensions of the CREED, composed and designed to further promulgate spiritual character among the lower ranks.

CREST OF A CIRCLE - Top or apex of a circle.

CRESCENT - A path of action that can be compared and paralleled to a HOOKING type of maneuver.

CRESCENT KICK - A method of kicking that resembles a HOOK KICK. Close examination will reveal that they are identical in application. ▼

CRITICAL DISTANCE - Crucial distance that can place you or your opponent within striking range. THIRD STAGE OF RANGE known as CONTACT PENETRATION.

CROSS CHECK - (1) Refers to crossing to the opposite side of your opponent's body, when pinning or striking him so that your action prevents him from retaliating. It literally concludes as a CROSS CHECK. (2) Diagonally checking an opponent's action so that his reaction or intended action cannot hit you, nor have access to a vulnerable area on your body.

CROSS DRAW POSITION - Refers to the tucking of a nunchaku (or other possible weapons), under a belt or section of clothing on the opposite side of the hand that plans to use it.

CROSS VS. DIRECT - These two terms have particular significance when referring to PUSHES and GRABS. A CROSS push or grab indicates that your opponent, who is facing you, is using his right hand to push or grab your right shoulder or chest. Your opponent's left hand to your left shoulder or chest would also apply. A DIRECT push or grab indicates that your opponent, who is facing you, is using his right hand to push or grab your left shoulder or chest. This would also apply if your opponent used his left hand to your right shoulder. When your opponent's hand and arm crosses over your body to make contact it is a CROSS push or grab. When your opponent pushes or grabs with the hand that is directly opposite you, it is a DIRECT push or grab. CROSS kicks serve a dual purpose in that they injure your opponent, as well as check his ability to retaliate.

CUBE MODEL - An outlined drawing of a box superimposed over a photo or drawing to explain angles and paths of travel more efficiently. It is a useful visual aid that enhances one's understanding of angles and paths of travel. See CONCEPTUAL BOX.

CUP & SAUCER - This term describes a specific formation that the hands conform to in order to prevent retaliation. You will notice, when observing this hand formation, that it resembles a waiter carrying a cup and saucer. An example of this can be found in the technique Dance of Darkness.

CUSHION - Generally refers to the use of a block to soften the effect of an opponent's strike. The block occurs away from your body so that the force of your opponent's strike dissipates prior to making, or not making contact with your body.

DANCER - Tournament slang for one who continuously bounces around.

DARK(NESS) - A term used in self-defense techniques, that refers to attacks initiated from your rear or flank. Because these moves stem from the unknown (areas which you can't see), the terms DARK or DARKNESS are used.

DEAD MOTION DECEPTION - Tactical use of illusion to make it appear that all motion is at a stand still. Then, from out of what appears to be nowhere, an intended strike is activated. Such unexpected action comes as a big surprise.

DEAD MOTION PRINCIPLE - A deceptive maneuver that is purposely designed to give your opponent the illusion that a portion of your body is totally inactive (or seems dead), and can do them no harm. A good example is the action that can stem out of arms that have been folded. For instance, if your left arm was folded on top of your right arm, and it remained motionless during the time your right hand executed a back knuckle strike to you opponent's solar plexus, your opponent would not react to your strike until he felt the blow. The fact that your left arm showed no life conditioned his mind to accept peace and tranquility. Not until experiencing the strike, would he have realized the consequence of your action.

DEAD SPACE - (1) The gaps between moves in a technique sequence. It can also be thought of as unused points on a circle, or circles, of motion. The filling of DEAD SPACE is the active use of the principle of CONTINUITY OF MOTION. This action is termed SEQUENTIAL FLOW. (2) Areas or zones of refuge where one can seek SANCTUARY. See ZONES OF SANCTUARY.

DECEPTIVE ACTION - The utilization of misleading, illusive, and feinting movements or gestures to deceive an opponent.

DECEPTIVE FEINTS - The purposeful conditioning of an opponent to insure a planned conditioned response.

DECEPTIVE GESTURES - Same as DECEPTIVE ACTION and FEINTS.

DECEPTIVE RHYTHM - Irregular sequential flow of timing purposely used to throw off an opponent's timing, and disrupt his flow of concentration. Another term for DECEPTIVE TIMING.

DECEPTIVE TIMING - Timing used to mislead an opponent, causing him to react prematurely, anticipating the opposite of your true intentions. It is that measure of time used when feinting. See DECEPTIVE RHYTHM.

DEFENSE - Protective moves designed to safeguard against injury.

DEFENSIVE OFFENSE - Execution of a move which is both protective to you and simultaneously injurious to the opponent.

DEFENSIVE PERSUASION - Refers to the forcing of an opponent to defend a particular area, in order to effectively create an opening elsewhere.

DEFINITIVE - A term that is used to describe moves that are explicit, absolute, and clear-cut when executed.

DEFLECT - To deviate the course of an attacking weapon.

DEGREE(S) - The (1) extent of one's injury, or (2) level(s) of achievement bestowed upon a Brown or Black Belt, as required in the BELT RANKING SYSTEM.

DELAYED MOVEMENT - A strategic combat technique employing a pause during a sequential flow of action. This strategy is purposefully used to alter the timing of a RHYTHMIC PATTERN, in order to baffle an opponent. RETARDED MOVEMENT also fits this description. Just as you must know your basic colors, in order to blend and mix them and your notes in music before arranging them into melodic tunes, so must you know RHYTHMIC PATTERNS in order to alter your timing to confuse your opponent.

DELETE - The elimination of a weapon and/or target within a technique sequence.

DEPARTURE - A term used in the title of some of the self-defense techniques that indicates the use of optimum angles of escape to assure a safe distance from your fallen opponent(s).

DEPTH DECEPTION - Conditioning your opponent to accept an established depth range, then making a switch that will lengthen or shorten that range when he least expects it.

DEPTH OF ACTION - The ability to extend the range of your offensive and defensive movements, when and where needed, to obtain maximum results from your efforts.

DEPTH PENETRATION - The concept of going beyond the point of contact when striking with a weapon.

DEPTH PERCEPTION - The ability to judge accurately the distances between objects and yourself. This ability enables one to gauge reaction time and speed with utmost precision and accuracy.

DEPTH ZONES - One of the categorical ZONES OF PROTECTION. It entails the protection of approximately seven depth zones. These are vertical zones viewed from the side.

DETAINING CHECK - A momentary block that occurs during the execution of, and as a result of the path of, a strike being delivered to a selected target. A ricochet punch is a good example of this principle. See OFFENSIVE CHECK or RICOCHETING BLOCKING STRIKE.

DETAINING STRIKE - A strike that is purposely locked out upon contact with the target, whereby it momentarily delays an opponent from instantly re-positioning himself for a counter attack. Lock outs of this nature prevent your opponent from regaining his point of origin and thus disallows him from functioning instantly.

DIAMOND STANCE - A type of stance where the knees are arched or curved out. This particular stance can be found in the LEAP OF DEATH, a self-defense technique that teaches you how to effectively use this stance as a vehicle employing two weapons at once.

DICTIONARY - (Refer to ANALOGY OF APPENDIX/DICTIONARY/ENCYCLOPEDIA).

DICTION OF MOTION - The ability to make each move of a sequential flow crisp and distinct. Just as you articulate words so can you articulate moves.

DIMENSION(S) - A term incorporating such aspects as height, width, and depth. It is one of the divisions of MOTION which when understood will give you a clearer picture of what motion is all about.

DIMENSIONAL STAGES OF ACTION - The viewing of the space or gap between you and an opponent from all aspects of height, width, depth, and direction, with regard to the distances that are necessary in maintaining, closing, controlling, and opening the gap. Each view or stage logically requires long, medium, and close range techniques while closing in on an opponent, or when covering out. Of particular interest is the staggering number of alternatives that exist when employing close range techniques. They include not only strikes, but various methods of CONTOURING, LOCKS and CHOKES, TWISTS, DISLOCATIONS and HOLDS, and TAKEDOWNS.

DIMENSIONAL ZONE CONCEPT - A concept created to teach students of American Kenpo to visualize their opponent's body divided into vertical and horizontal zones (sections) as viewed from the front, side, or back. This allows the student to subdivide an opponent into four basic zones — height, width, depth, and zones of obscurity. This knowledge can then be used to restrict your opponent's dimensions, or keep them in check. Controlling your opponent's actions by restricting the use and versatility of his dimensions (ANGLE OF CANCELLATION), makes retaliation on the part of your opponent considerably more difficult.

DIPPING - Any move that drops before rising during its path of action.

DIPPING CHECK - A type of check that is built into an offensive strike. The check occurs on the downward (dipping) motion of your action just prior to making contact with your target on the high side of your curve. See BLOCKING CHECK.

DIRECT ROTATION - Circular or torquing action that is completed in a single twirl.

DIRECTED BLOCKADE - (1) The control and steering of one opponent into another as a barrier to obstruct the efforts of both attacking opponents. (2) The use of environmental objects as a barrier to obstruct the efforts of your opponent. These environmental objects are skillfully directed and guided as part of one's strategy to defeat an opponent.

DIRECTION(S) - A term that refers to front, back, side (left and right), up and down, above and below. It is another division of MOTION that aids your understanding and gauging of offensive and defensive potentials.

DIRECTIONAL CHANGE - The ability to switch or alter directions of a weapon or movement while keeping the momentum of your body flowing constantly, and without interrupting the initial motion. See DIRECTIONAL SWITCH.

DIRECTIONAL HARMONY - Having all of your action moving in the same direction. This principle aids in obtaining maximum results. It is a requirement when executing BODY MOMENTUM that residually triggers BACK-UP-MASS.

DIRECTIONAL HARMONY VS. DIRECT OPPOSITES - These are two methods of generating power. DIRECTIONAL HARMONY requires that all body mass travel in the same direction when following a line or path of action. Power can also stem from motion that is split into DIRECT OPPOSITES. In this situation, one force going in any direction can enhance the force of an action that is moving away, or directly opposite from it. This type of action can be compared to the snapping of a whip. A whip can generate incredible energy provided that the snap and pull during its execution are directly opposite from each other.

DIRECTIONAL SWITCH - A method of changing direction while keeping the momentum of your body in constant flow. The basic idea is to redirect, not interrupt the motion started.

DISCIPLINE - The ability to enforce upon oneself a pattern of positive behavior so that it can become ingrained and a habitual part of your life. Habitual behavior is a necessary ingredient if you wish to train diligently, consistently, and successfully.

DISENGAGE - To separate from an opponent. To release an opponent after having controlled the gap between the two of you.

DISLOCATION - The separation of two bones from the joint that links them together. The displacement of a bone joint from its proper position.

DISPLACEMENT - To dislodge, move, uproot, or replace.

DISPLACEMENT OF DISTANCE - The reestablishing of range via foot maneuvers.

DISTANCE - It is the degree or amount of separation between you and your opponent(s).

DISTRACTION - Intentional move or moves used in freestyle or combat to divert the attention and disrupt the concentration of an opponent. Such moves can create openings that can allow you favorable access to vital targets. See DECEPTIVE MOVES and ACTION.

DISTURB - Use of strategic movements to disrupt and upset an opponent's thoughts, balance, posture, or action.

DISHARMONY OF FORCE - Moves that are in opposition to DIRECTIONAL HARMONY. The splitting of force in various directions which greatly lessens the effect of your technique.

DIVER - Tournament slang for someone who puts on an act. See ACTOR.

DIVERSIFIED ANGLE OF ATTACK - The ability to commence an attack from one angle, and be able to readily switch into still another angle without disturbing the flow of motion, especially when only one hand is employed. Example: a punch to your opponent's jaw can unhesitatingly be converted into a stiff arm lifting forearm strike under his chin. In the case of two hands, alternate action from two or more angles while striking to the same target, or two separate targets, are still considered DIVERSIFIED ANGLE(S) OF ATTACK. Refer to DIRECTIONAL CHANGE and DIRECTIONAL SWITCH.

DIVERSIFIED ANGLE OF COVER - Refers to changing directions while covering out; not getting into the habit of covering out in one direction.

DIVERSIFIED ANGLE OF RETREAT - Same as DIVERSIFIED ANGLE OF COVER.

DIVERSIFIED ANGLE OF VIEW - Increased number of perspectives beyond the normal three points of view. This entails the viewpoint of additional bystanders, so that all angles of observation are considered. Having just a third point of view is not enough. Observing your opponent from additional viewpoints via reflections on mirrors, plate glass, and shiny objects can prove exceedingly beneficial.

DIVERSIFIED EXTENSIONS - Refers to the astonishing number of alternatives that can stem from various points of origin. (1) They can originate from a single action, or can spontaneously materialize periodically throughout the course of your sequential flow of action. The topic encompasses the internalized or instinctive use of alternate natural weapons and targets. (2) The ability to randomly change a natural weapon, and instinctively choose an opening that will achieve the greatest effect; as in a block, altering into a chop to the neck, a hammerfist to the jaw, a knuckle rake across the nose, or a finger slice across the eyes of your opponent, or any other strike that can be appropriately used to a target that is open.

DIVERSIFIED FLOW OF ACTION - Altering the timing of your sequential flow of action so that these rhythmic changes keep your opponent baffled. See DECEPTIVE RHYTHM and TIMING.

DIVERSIFIED TARGETS - Striking various targets to insure multiple effects.

DIVES - Unique methods that employ springs and flips. The moves are quite exaggerated, and are used to (1) avoid an attack, (2) work in conjunction with an attack, or (3) can be combined as a defense and offense. Because they are unique, DIVES are categorized separately. The chief characteristic of a Dive is the height levels of the head and feet. In a DIVE, the head lunges forward followed by the feet. At a certain period of the DIVE, the height of the feet raises above the level of the head. It is this relationship of height — the feet being higher than the head — that separates a DIVE from a JUMP.

DOMESTIC FORM - Slang for a form of short duration.

DOUBLE CHECK - It is the execution of a single, simultaneous, or alternating delivery that restrains, hinders, or prevents an opponent from taking action from more than one leverage point. ▼

DOUBLE COVER OUT - A single crossover step through reverse, with an additional step through reverse, to reassure greater distance between you and your opponent(s). This gives a greater cover position because, in the process of maneuvering, your vision encompasses two 180 degree angle scans which give you a 360 degree total scanning advantage.

DOUBLE FACTOR - It entails utilizing dual movements to defend yourself. These moves can incorporate any combination of blocks, parries, and checks. It also refers to sophisticated moves which are dually defensive and offensive. REVERSE MOTION is an integral part of this concept.

DOUBLE STRIKE - The use of two natural weapons to simultaneously strike two separate targets where, more often than not, one of the strikes is residually used as a check.

DOJO - The Japanese term for school or training hall.

DOWN-SIDE OF THE CIRCLE - Basically refers to contact being made after passing the apex or crest of a circle. It is this action that determines it as being a HOOK.

DRAG - The sliding of one foot toward the other while either moving forward, backward, or to the side.

DRAG KICK - The sliding of one foot to the other prior to the opposite (stationary) foot executing a kick.

DRAG STEP - The sliding of one foot forward, backward, or to the side before having the opposite foot step away from it. It is one of the four categorical methods of SHUFFLING.

DRAGON - A symbol used in Kenpo to represent spiritual strength, humility, and self restraint. It is that ultimate stage that all Kenpo practitioners should try to achieve.

DRAW-IN - Combat strategy to lure an opponent within range so that contact penetration can be effectively applied.

DROP(PING) - A rapid descent of your body while simultaneously delivering a strike. Its execution greatly contributes to the principle of MARRIAGE OF GRAVITY, where the ability to use the weight of your body becomes a distinct advantage.

DUCKING - Sudden descent to avoid being hit. This involves an instant drop of body height in order to dodge or avoid a strike. See BOBBING.

E

ECONOMY OF MOTION - Entails choosing the best available weapon for the best available angle, to insure reaching the best available target in the least amount of time, while still obtaining the desired result. Any movement that takes less time to execute, but still causes the effect intended. Any movement that inhibits or does not actively enhance the effect intended is categorized as WASTED MOTION.

EDGE EFFECT - Another method of employing SURFACE CONCENTRATION. It too is concerned with the impact force between weapon and target, and the resulting stresses that occur. It follows the principle of a pin or a nail, 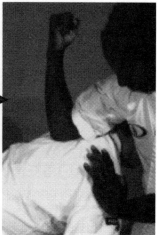 where the surface of the natural weapon being used is concentrated in order to have a more penetrating effect on the target. See PIN POINT EFFECT and SURFACE CONCENTRATION. A good example of this can be found in the technique DEFYING THE STORM.

EIGHT CONSIDERATIONS - The eight factors involved in freestyle or combat that must be considered or anticipated in order to be victorious. Listed in the order of their importance, they are: (1) environment, (2) range, (3) positions, (4) maneuvers, (5) targets, (6) natural weapons, (7) blocks, and (8) cover.

EIGHTEEN HAND MOVEMENTS - The original number of hand movements first developed at the Shaolin Temple in China to defend or attack an opponent. These moves supposedly formed the foundation of Shaolin Boxing.

ELECTRONIC DETONATOR THEORY - The idea that the internal explosion of all movements should be activated as rapidly as an electronic detonator used to trigger dynamite or other types of explosives. See FUSE and PLUNGER THEORIES.

ELONGATED CIRCLES - The lengthening of circular movements so that the paths in which they travel follow a more flattened arc. This maneuver shortens the time of action, and because of the modified angle of travel, is able to strike the target with greater speed, penetration, and force.

EMBRYONIC BASICS - Simple basic movements that are generally single in action and purpose. Although primitive in nature, they form the basic roots of Kenpo.

EMBRYONIC MOVES - Same as EMBRYONIC BASICS.

EMBRYONIC STAGE - Refers to the very primitive stage of learning.

EMPTY HANDS - A term associated with all Martial Art systems that employ only natural body weapons while defending or attacking.

ENGAGE - To come together; to make contact with an opponent.

ENGINEER OF MOTION - That stage in a student's study where he not only can dissect motion, inspect it, understand it, and reassemble it like a mechanic, but also build on and from it. At this stage he can rearrange, fuse, or create more sophisticated principles. These may stem from a combination of existing principles, but nevertheless, through the engineer's unique perspective and tailoring, Kenpo's principles continue to expand.

ENHANCED STRIKE - A second weapon, used as an immediate follow-up, pounding on top of the first weapon that was employed.

Hammering is an example of a Enhanced Strike

ENVIRONMENT - Conditions that confront us on a daily basis. It involves social and cultural conditions, objects around us, thoughts that are in us, condition of our bodies, weather conditions, ability of your opponent, objects which an opponent may use, and all other factors that influence our chances of survival. It is everything around you, on you, and in you at the time of confrontation.

ENVIRONMENTAL AWARENESS - The ability to observe daily conditions and surroundings, and make on-the-spot decisions to either avoid danger, or take advantage of the opportunities offered.

ENVIRONMENTAL CONDITIONS - Existing conditions when involved in combat or tournament freestyle, which include: rules of a particular tournament, weather conditions, time of day, number of persons involved, character identity, general surroundings, layout, floor plan, terrain, and most important, your state of mind at the time of confrontation.

ENVIRONMENTAL OBJECTS - Same as ENVIRONMENTAL WEAPONS.

ENVIRONMENTAL WEAPONS - Objects, from your general surroundings, that can be used as weapons — bottles, chairs, ash trays, stanchions, walls, utensils, etc.

EQUATION FORMULA - This is a special formula that one can follow to develop specific, practical, and logical fighting patterns. The formula allows you a more conclusive basis for negotiating your alternate actions. It reads as follows: To any given base, whether it is a single move or a series of movements, you can (1) prefix it — add a move or moves before it; (2) suffix it — add a move or moves after it; (3) insert — add a simultaneous move with, the already established sequence (this move can be used as a (a) pinning check — using pressure against an opponent's weapons to nullify their delivery, or (b) positioned check — where you place the hand or leg in a defensive position or angle to minimize entry to your vital areas; (4) rearrange — change the sequence of the moves, (5) alter the — (a) weapon, (b) target, (c) both weapon and target; (6) adjust the — (a) range, (b) angle of execution (which affects width and height), (c) both angle of execution and range; (7) regulate the — (a) speed, (b) force, (c) both speed and force, (d) intent and speed; and (8) delete — exclude a move or moves from the sequence.

EVASIVE MOVE - Any move that avoids an attack without blocking.

EXAGGERATED STEP - A simplified term used in Kenpo to describe a kick or stomp.

EXHALE - The expulsion of air during the breathing process.

EXHALE VS. INHALE - While both parts of the breathing process are important to the martial artist, each must be viewed in terms of its individual advantages and disadvantages. The advantage of exhaling is that it helps to stabilize your base during the execution of your moves, and can increase the power of your action as a result. The disadvantage arises when the expulsion of air is not properly timed with the execution of your strike. The timing of your strike and expulsion of air must be in perfect "sync" to get the full benefit from your strike. Inhaling has the disadvantage of buoyancy and instability. See BUOYANCY. When your body is unsettled and unbalanced your power is greatly reduced. The advantage when inhaling, however, is that buoyancy can become an asset when moving about or covering out. It seems that the body is lighter and much more free to move about when buoyant. Another benefit can be had by secretly inhaling, retaining the air in you, and then springing into action. Evidence of this special manner of breathing is not apparent to your opponent, and when an attack is launched, the stored air causes the body to explode into action. Explosions of this nature greatly accelerate delivery, and if the timing is precise, the benefits are rewarding.

EXPANDED AWARENESS - As one's proficiency increases his mind is proportionately more perceptive and conscious of the details surrounding him.

EXPANDING DISTANCE - Another term describing the increase of range between you and an opponent. See OPEN(ING) THE GAP.

EXPLOSIVE ACTION - Instantaneous action or reaction that ignites and bursts from inside out with repetitive succession.

EXPLOSIVE PRESSURE - Bursting aggressive action that keeps constant force on an opponent, thus preventing him from setting himself up to retaliate.

EXTEMPORANEOUS - Done on the spur of the moment, impromptu, improvised. Growing out of the occasion: unexpected. Motion becomes extemporaneous when the SPONTANEOUS STAGE is learned. Freestyle is a partial test of extemporaneous motion.

EXTENDED OUTWARD BLOCK - A type of block that is delivered out, up, and away from the body. It is a block used at medium range.

EXTENSION(S) - (1) The straightening of a flexed limb. (2) Additions to the standard belt techniques.

EXTERNAL PHYSICAL WEAKNESS - Self-induced weakening of the body imposed by outward forces such as steam, fire, etc., to humble the soul.

EXTERNAL SYSTEMS - One of two schools of thought concerning the development of power through proper breathing. Proponents of this school advocate active and forceful methods of breathing, while their counterparts feel that breathing should be kept calm. See INTERNAL SYSTEMS.

EYELESS SIGHT - The ability to identify printed figures, colors, and objects with just the surface of the skin—not the eyes. A type of PARANORMAL SENSITIVITY.

F

FACE EACH OTHER - (1) Where two individuals face each other while awaiting further command. (2) A preparatory command given prior to commencing a freestyle match where both opponents are opposite each other prior to dropping into a fighting stance.

FADE-OUT - To retreat or back away from the action you are involved in. See COVER OUT.

FALLING - A type of BODY MANEUVER where the body drops to the ground: (1) to avoid being hit (defense), or (2) after being hit or thrown (offense). This maneuver basically entails the feet remaining on the same spot; however, this is not the case when thrown to the ground. Analyzing it technically, FALLING is an exaggerated method of RIDING an attack. It entails going with the force as you land on your back, side, or stomach. Although RIDING normally occurs while remaining on your feet it can be combined with a FALL.

FAMILY GROUPINGS - Movements that stem from the same source, position, point of origin, or point of reference. Although these moves stem from the same point of origin, their methods of execution vary according to circumstance. Applying this concept teaches how the first two moves of your initial action could be viewed as Mother/Father moves. Action stemming from Mother/Father moves produce Brother/Sister moves. Secondary, but similarly structured positions, produce Aunt/Uncle moves. Moves stemming from them produce Cousin moves, etc.

FAMILY RELATED MOVES - The use of the same move or moves against a number of predicaments that are basically similar in context, but so often overlooked as being similar in principle. For example, the answer to a wrist grab can (via slight alteration) be the same answer to a hair or lapel grab. The basic action is to control the opponent's wrist while striking against the joint of his elbow. The answer to a "rear bear hug", arms free, can also work if the arms were pinned, or if the hug was converted into a "Full Nelson".

FAMILY TREE - A genealogical chart of Mr. Parker's first and second generation Black Belts (Last updated in 1980). See Volume I of *"Infinite Insights into Kenpo"* by Ed Parker.

FAN - A term used in self-defense techniques referring to circular parries.

FAST - Generally refers to the speed of your physical action.

FAST VS. QUICK - While fast generally refers to the speed of your physical action, quick equates with mental speed, or the ability to think rapidly.

FEATHERS - A term used in self-defense techniques that refers to the hair.

FEEL - A word used to describe the foot or hand as it slides from one point to another. In the case of the foot the concept teaches you to move your foot back very lightly so that you literally feel the ground, when sliding in the hope of overcoming possible obstacles.

FEINT - A misleading move or gesture used to deceive an opponent. See DECEPTIVE MOVES.

FIGHTING EQUATION - Same as EQUATION FORMULA.

FIGHTING POSITION - A defensive posture used prior to or during combat, as well as in tournament sparring. It may be coupled with an assumed stance, or formed when protecting yourself while on   the ground, on the beach, in bed, seated in a chair, etc.

FIGHTING SENTENCE - Combined movements of hands and feet, that are used defensively or offensively in a sequence.

FIGHTING STANCE - Same as FIGHTING POSITION.

FIGURE EIGHT - A path of travel that one or two hands (or feet) may follow which resembles the number eight. When employing this pattern of action the number eight may be used upright or on its side.

FILET - A special Kenpo term used to describe a particular method of applying the blade of a knife when involved in a knife fight to peel or slice away layers of flesh.

FILLING THE GAP - Generally refers to occupying the distance that exists between you and your opponent more fully.

FINAL POSITION - The concluding move of a sequence.

FINGER SET I - A required set for Blue Belt done from a Horse Stance. It contains fourteen methods of utilizing the fingers.

FINGER SET II - A set containing fourteen methods of utilizing the fingers while moving through various stance changes.

FIRE - A command used to trigger a strike or to commence action.

FIRST COUSIN/SECOND COUSIN MOVES - These moves can be best understood by discussing Family Groupings. Family Groupings are movements that are similar in context, and/or movements that can stem from the same source, origin, or reference point. They are somewhat related to Associated Moves, and are often referred to as Family Related Moves.

Think of your family structure. From your point of view you are the central figure, and the family kinships are in relationship to you (your mother, your brother, your cousin etc.). The central core of your family consists of yourself, your parents, and your brothers and sisters. Your extended family consists of your more distant relatives with whom you are less familiar (your aunts, uncles, cousins, and in-laws).

In self-defense you are, once again, the central figure. "Me", "my", and "I" are the most important pronouns. You must think of yourself first; think of what you must do to protect yourself; contemplate the benefits of such movement for yourself,etc. In Kenpo we can think of the initial defensive positioning of your arms as father/mother movements. A left inward block would be a father movement and the positioning of your right arm would be the mother movement (right arm hanging naturally at your side, cocked at the hip, cocked at the ear, etc.). It is the initial move that protects you. Just as your parents come first so do the protective blocks. Thus, a technique such as Dance of Death has a left inward block as its father, and the naturally hanging right arm is its mother. Flashing Wings, likewise, uses a left inward block as its father, and the cocked right arm at the hip as its mother. The technique, Five Swords utilizes a right inward block as its father movement and the left checking hand as its mother movement.

In a crisis, your true brothers and sisters quickly come to your aid; likewise, after your initial block, you can counterattack with your right or left arm. If your counterattack is executed with the opposite arm of the one that blocked, then it is a brother movement. If you counterattack with the same arm that blocked, then it is a sister movement. And so, the techniques Dance of Death and Flashing Wings, after their initial father/mother movement, counterattack with a brother strike; Five Swords counterattacks with a sister movement.

Therefore, techniques such as Dance of Death, Thundering Hammers, and Sleeper may be seen to be Family Related. They use the same father/Mother movements and counterattack with a Brother strike. The techniques Attacking Mace and Flashing Wings are Family Related to each other because they have the same father/mother movement, and the same brother hand is utilized to counterattack. Dance of Death and attacking Mace both use left inward blocks as their father movements. These father movements are brothers to each other. Therefore, the right hand counterattacks of the techniques are "cousin" to each other.

The left inward parry used in Leaping Crane is very much like a left inward block. It is said to be "cousin" to the inward block. The techniques initial right hand counter is then "second cousin" to techniques such as Dance of Death or Attacking Mace. The ultimate purpose of Family Groupings is to provide spontaneous action through association and familiarity; to help free you from a series of prearranged ideas, and to unite them as one single idea with associated variations. For example, the techniques Attacking Mace, Flashing Wings, and Circling the Storm all have the same father/mother movement, as well as the same brother counterattack. They may then be used as one single idea that may be varied as the situation dictates. Your ability to extend the relationships between family groups will create larger and larger families, and thus fewer single unifying ideas, with a larger number of variations, creating greater spontaneity.

The study of Family Groupings can enhance your spontaneity tremendously. Remember that Family Related Moves should be tailored to you. If you perceive a logical association of movements, then you can group them; if that grouping makes you more spontaneous, and it works, then use it. You may also, through your training, discover aunts/uncles, orphans, adopted moves etc... as stated above. Please remember that Family Groupings was never meant to be an all-encompassing model for the system. Its use should not be stretched so far that it becomes trivial and nonfunctional.

FIRST LINE OF DEFENSE - The furthermost part of your defensive posture (but closest to your opponent) that is initially used as your first ZONE OF PROTECTION.

FIRST POINT OF VIEW - It is what you observe from your point of view. Your understanding or awareness of what is before you, what action you are initiating, and how your opponent is responding to your action.

FITTING - Applying a natural weapon shaped to fit the target being struck. It's like fitting pieces in a puzzle. The effective penetration of a strike is greatly enhanced when it and its target are fittingly matched. This principle is known as the PUZZLE PRINCIPLE. It, too, is categorized as a method of CONTOURING.

FIXED SLICE - Describes a hand that is rigid, firm, and stable when executing a slice.

FLAILING METHODS - Methods used when swinging one or both ends of the nunchaku.

FLAME - Part of the International Karate Championship symbol (logo). It is symbolic of perpetual friendship and brotherhood which, if kindled by all Karate systems, will glow with a brilliance each year. Its beauty can be paralleled with the art — graceful and useful, yet deadly when touched. The three tips of the flame represent the three stages of learning — primitive, mechanical, and spontaneous.

FLEXIBILITY - (1) Means to increase the range of motions which are possible in a joint. (2) Also refers to freedom of thought and action, so that instinctive and extemporaneous responses can randomly and effectively take place.

FLICKING SLICE - A specialized method of slicing with the finger(s) that employs a whipping action to complete its function. Depth of action also occurs during the whip.

FLOWERY - Generally refers to fancy movements that look pretty, but fall short of practical use.

FLUID MOVEMENTS - Moves that flow with continuity, and that contribute to ECONOMY OF MOTION.

FLURRY - Explosive and fast exchange of blows, strikes, kicks, etc.

FLURRY FIGHTER - One who uses a series of fast techniques, and then waits. (Tournament slang.)

FOCUS - Is the result of the entire body working as a unit at the very instant a target is struck. The concentration of mind (knowledge), breath, strength, and methods of execution must unite as one in conjunction with body momentum, torque, gravitational marriage, timing, speed, penetration, etc. It must be remembered that it is not just the concentration of weapon meeting target, but the entire body meeting the target as one unit that fully defines the term FOCUS.

FOOT MAN - One who primarily uses his feet when competing. (Tournament slang.)

FOOT MANEUVERS - Methods using the feet and legs to transport your body from one ground point to another while traveling in a multitude of directions. Examples — step throughs, crossovers, twist outs, shuffles (step drag, drag step, push drag, pull drag), jumps, and dives.

FORCE - Use of energy and power with obvious effort. When viewed it often looks as if it is accompanied by exertion.

FORCE FIELD - Refers to confining your movements within the aura of your body, so that the strength and effectiveness of your actions are significantly increased. Confining your movements within close proximity of your body for the purpose of controlling your actions. It is this controlled balance of extension and bracing angle that adds to the strength and power of your actions.

FORM - Is literally a short story of motion. It consists of basic movements of offense and defense incorporated into a dance-like routine for purposes of exercising, training without a partner, or training at home. It is an index of movements that gives specific answers, as well as speculative interpretations to combat situations.

FORM I - There is a Short Form I and a Long Form I. Short Form I is a required Form for Yellow Belt. Long Form I is required for Orange Belt.

FORM II - There is a Short Form II and a Long Form II. Short Form II is required for Purple Belt. Long Form II is a requirement for Blue Belt.

FORM III - There is a Short Form III and a Long Form III. Short Form III is required for Green Belt. Long Form III is a requirement for 3rd Degree Brown.

FORM IV - A requirement for 1st Degree Brown.

FORM V - A requirement for 2nd Degree Black.

FORM VI - A requirement for 3rd Degree Black.

FORM VII - A requirement for 4th Degree Black.

FORM VIII - A requirement for 5th Degree Black.

FORM INDICATORS - The use of hand signals to signify the FORM you are about to demonstrate. Same as SIGNIFY or HAND SIGNALS.

FORMULATE - The combining of moves into a systematized order which, when properly organized, develops into a logical and practical sequential arrangement.

FORM-THE-LINE - A command given to students to form a single line to perform techniques as a means of practice. See TECHNIQUE LINE.

FORMULATION PHASE - This is PHASE III of the analytical process of dissecting a technique. This PHASE involves the actual application of your newly found alternatives to the original IDEAL or fixed technique. Knowing what can additionally happen within the framework of the fixed technique, teaches you how to apply your variable answers to a free and changing environment. This ultimate process of combat training can be learned by using the EQUATION FORMULA for fighting. See EQUATION FORMULA.

FORWARD BOW - A stance that can easily be initiated from a NEUTRAL BOW by rotating on the vertical axis so that the rear hip is even with the forward hip, the rear leg is straightened, and 60% of your body weight is transferred to the forward leg. The formation of this stance can give you greater reach, enhance your power, and can effectively be used as a leg check, buckle, bracing angle, or break.

FOUR STAGES OF RANGE - Stages of range, within the "gap", that are crucial in combat. Listed in order of proximity they are (1) OUT OF CONTACT, (2) WITHIN CONTACT, (3) CONTACT PENETRATION, and (4) CONTACT MANIPULATION. Refer to all four under their separate heading. Also review the DIMENSIONAL STAGES OF ACTION.

FRAMING - A method of CONTOURING where a limb of the body symmetrically forms around another part of the body to establish what literally looks like a frame around the subject. See ANGLE MATCHING and SILHOUETTING.

FREESTYLE - A term used in Karate for sparring. As in boxing, it is a combination of offensive and defensive moves used extemporaneously. To state it differently, it is a combative method of freely expressing yourself physically.

FREEZE FRAME - A method used to isolate a move in order to make study more exacting.

FRICTIONAL PULL - A method of pulling and unbalancing an opponent with the use of friction. When anticipated, responses caused by such action can conveniently set an opponent up for additional counters. Friction caused by scraping, hooking, and pulling can induce pain to a much wider area on an opponent's body. The effect of multiple pain becomes an additional asset in that it occupies your opponent's mind to a point where he is not apt to think of retaliation. See CONTOURING since FRICTIONAL PULL falls under this heading.

FRICTIONAL SCRAPE - An aggressive scrape that digs into the target, and augments the initial impact of the movement.

FRONT CROSSOVER - A type of foot maneuver which involves the back foot crossing over and in front of the forward leg, or the forward leg moving over and in front of the rear leg, when moving forward or back.

FULCRUM(ING) - Specific areas of the body that are used as supporting leverage points, to help increase the effectiveness of our actions. See LEVERAGING.

FULL CONTACT - Term primarily used to describe professional freestylists where actual contact, when hitting, is acceptable. Unlike American boxing, which allows only fists to strike above the waist, Full Contact fighters are allowed to use the feet, knees, and elbows as additional weapons to areas above and below the waist.

FUSE THEORY - The idea that internal explosion, when executing your movements, must not be compared to a fuse on a stick of dynamite. It takes time for the fuse to burn before it can set off a stick of dynamite. Internal explosion must be instantaneous for it to be effective. See ELECTRONIC DETONATOR and PLUNGER THEORIES.

FUSION - The uniting together as one. See BODY FUSION.

GAP - The existing distance between, or that separates, you and your opponent.

GAUGING LEG - The leg used to alter the distance between your opponent and yourself for purposes of offense or defense.

GAUGING OF DISTANCE - The ability to systematically regulate the distance between opponent and self for purposes of defense or attack.

GEOMETRIC LINE - The concept of visualizing a line that a weapon (natural or otherwise) or block must travel to reach the desired target. Line, in Kenpo terms, is one-dimensional, and refers to the course of a single point on a block or strike as it travels toward a target.

GEOMETRIC PATH - The concept of visualizing an entire limb being used to block or strike with, rather than just a portion of it. This concept allows a greater margin for error, since it is the entire path of the action that you are to contemplate using. It works on the "SQUEEGEE PRINCIPLE" where it's not the outer ends of a limb that are utilized, but the entire area between the ends. The outer boundaries of the action form the geometric lines, while the area between the outer boundaries constitutes the path. Instead of following geometric lines, we should all learn to employ geometric paths. It insures better protection. This principle can also be paralleled to the concept of UPPER AND LOWER CASE.

GEOMETRIC SYMBOL CONCEPT - The use of circles, squares, triangles, etc. as visual and mental training aids while learning the angles and paths one must take when defending oneself, or when attacking an opponent.

GHOST IMAGE - The visualization of your previous position and location, used to analyze the shift (repositioning) of axis points, in order to determine the best course of action.

GI - Training uniform used by Kenpo, Karate, Judo, and Aikido practitioners.

GIFT - A term used in self-defense techniques that refers to defenses against unfriendly hand-shakes.

GLANCING - A method of striking that is similar to a slice. The major difference is that the depth of penetration is much greater. It does not skim the surface of the target, but makes a deep penetration.

GOUGE(ING) - The thrusting of a thumb into an eye for the purpose of forcing it out.

GRABBER - One who constantly grabs his opponent's gi as a means of distraction. (Tournament slang.)

GRAB(BING) - To seize an opponent by a sudden grasp. The grasp entails clutching and snatching an opponent with sudden vigor.

GRADING - See BELT RANKING SYSTEM.

GRADUATED DEPTHS - (1) Imaginary depth zones that are viewed from the flank (profile). (2) Distances that occur between you and your opponent when engaged in combat. These depth gaps are critical if defense or offense are to be insured.

GRAFTED PRINCIPLE - Is the combining of several principles within the flow of a single action. As an example, a strike may start with a hammering motion, but conclude with a thrusting action without disturbing the natural flow of the executed move. The term also refers to combining self-defense techniques without disruption in their completed or uncompleted state.

GRAFTED TECHNIQUE - The blending of one technique, completed or not, into that of another without disrupting the continuation of your action. The transition occurs without disruption to the flow of either technique, or series of techniques.

GRAND TOTAL - Complete summation of your overall effectiveness that stems from unifying all principles concerned.

GRAVITATIONAL CHECK(S) - A form of CONTOURING where parts of an arm or leg rest on a particular surface area on an opponent's body, and prevent him from obtaining height and leverage. This restriction can detain or prevent an opponent from taking action that can be a threat. Such action generally occurs after the execution of a bracing check, where a vertical drop is additionally applied to pin down the height zone of an opponent even further.

GRAVITATIONAL MARRIAGE - The uniting of mind, breath and strength while simultaneously dropping your body weight along with the execution of your natural weapon(s). Timing all of these factors with the dropping of your body weight greatly adds to the force of your strikes. This combined action literally causes a marriage with gravity, and makes vertical use of BODY MOMENTUM while employing the dimension of HEIGHT.

GRAVY MOVEMENTS - A slang term used to describe COMPOUNDING A TECHNIQUE and MOVEMENTS OF PUNCTUATION. It refers to additional application that can stem out of the natural flow of motion in a form or a prescribed self-defense technique. They add flavor to your action, therefore, the term GRAVY. Such moves may not always be obvious in a form or prescribed self-defense technique, but are always within reach of the skilled practitioner. These moves are also known as "HIDDEN MOVES". They definitely add to ones overall knowledge of the "ALPHABETS OF MOTION".

GREATER ANGLE OF MOBILITY - A multitude of degrees or paths of approach that are void of encumbrances.

GUARD - Defensive positioning of the arms and legs in preparation for an attack. See FIGHTING POSITION.

GUARDED POSITIONS - Pre-set positional checks that can be altered to protect specifically designed postures of your choice.

GUIDED ANGLE OF DELIVERY - Utilization of parts of your or your opponent's body to help align and guide your weapon to the target of your choice. This method of contouring has a direct bearing on insuring accuracy. Constant contact with your or your opponent's body is necessary to insure accuracy when applying this method of contouring.

GUIDED COLLISION - The colliding of two or more assailants through the effective use of strategic manipulation.

GUIDELINING - A contact method of CONTOURING where an entire surface area is used to guide your natural weapon to its target. Contrary to TRACKING it follows a path of action.

GUIDING - Anything that points one in the right direction. The contour of the body is instrumental in accurately directing your strikes to specific targets. See AIMING.

HABITUAL BEHAVIOR - Advocates of the Martial Arts who continue to follow the same trend or pattern for good or bad.

HALF-FIST - A specific formation of the hand that entails clenching the fist part way. Clenching occurs at the second joint of each of the fingers. When executing this natural weapon it is the second joint of four of the fingers (thumb excluded), that makes contact with the target. See LEOPARD PUNCH.

HAMMER FIST - A natural weapon of the hand that is formed by clenching your fist totally. Strikes are done with either side of the fist (thumb or knife edge), and not with the joints of the knuckles. When viewing its execution, the action resembles the motions used when striking with a hammer.

HAMMERING - A particular method of striking which resembles the action of a hammer pounding a nail from various angles.

HAND-HELD METHODS - This refers to the various ways in which you can hold a nunchaku to effectively strike with it.

HAND MAN - One who primarily uses his hands when competing. (Tournament slang.)

HANDSPEAR - A specific term describing the finger tips when used like a spear.

HANDSWORD - A natural weapon of the hand that is formed by keeping the hand open with the fingers extended and joined, slightly bent, and thumb tucked in. When employed, it is either the thumb or knife edge portion of the hand that makes contact with the target of your choice.

HARD - Generally refers to moves that are executed with total power. It is another term used to describe major moves; hard hitting moves; moves that cause devastation.

HARD STYLE - A system that advocates power with every action.

HARM - To hurt, cause injury, or damage. See HURT.

HARMONIOUS MOVEMENTS - A pleasing arrangement of movements that contain continuity and economy of motion.

HARMONIZED POWER - All forces of power in unison.

HARMONY WITH THE MIND - Same as MENTAL HARMONY.

HARNESSING THE FORCE - The gathering and harmonizing of all principles, during a particular move or sequence of movements, in order to produce maximum power. As students learn to properly and fully adapt principles to their body type, they invariably learn to employ their energy with 100% efficiency and power.

HARNESSING YOUR ENERGY - Same as HARNESSING THE FORCE.

HEAD HUNTER - One who constantly strikes to the head with either hand or foot. (Tournament slang.)

HEAVY FOOT - One who is a strong kicker. (Tournament slang.)

HEEL HOOK KICK - A natural weapon of the foot that makes contact with the heel after passing the apex of the circle in which it travels.

HEEL/KNEE LINE - Method of determining the proper depth of a neutral bow and arrow stance. This is determined by turning both feet straight ahead, then kneeling to the ground on the rear knee so that when it is smartly and naturally placed on the ground it is on the same line (from 3 o'clock to 9 o'clock) as the heel of the forward foot.

HEIGHT DECEPTION - Conditioning your opponent to accept an established height pattern, then altering the pattern when he least expects it.

HEIGHT-WIDTH-DEPTH - Three important dimensions that are essential to understanding the scientific classifications of the Martial Arts.

HEIGHT ZONES - One of the divisions of the DIMEN-SIONAL ZONE THEORY. Zones related to this division encompass protection or attack on three levels. These levels are viewed horizontally — from the head to the solar plexus, the solar plexus to the groin, and the groin to the feet. See HORIZONTAL ZONES.

HIDDEN MOVES - Dormant moves that remain concealed until you activate them within the sequential flow of your self-defense technique. These moves have always existed; however, until the IDEAL phase of your self-defense technique is internalized you cannot effectively include them as part of your WHAT IF phase of knowledge. It is knowing how to compound the techniques that enables you to bring these hidden moves to the surface. To state it differently, HIDDEN MOVES are sophisticated additions that can be readily inserted within the flow of a prescribed technique. Although potential for these "moves within moves" is inherent in each technique, they are excluded for beginners, and will remain hidden until the student is sophisticated enough for their introduction. Technically, the use of HIDDEN MOVES is the same as COMPOUNDING a technique.

HINGE - The principle point of pivot.

"HIT AND GO" - Immediate departure after employing the last strike of a technique sequence.

HOLDS - To grasp or clutch someone to keep him from escaping.

HOOF - A term used in self-defense techniques that symbolizes a horse's hoof and the effects it can produce in injuring someone.

HOOK - The execution of a natural weapon that makes contact with its target after passing the apex of the circle in which it travels. In short, contact is made on the down-side, and not the upside of the circle in which your weapon travels. When delivering your weapon in the manner described, the position and angle in which it travels generally causes the weapon being used to catch or fasten itself to the target being struck.

HOP - A foot maneuver involving moving forward, backward, or to the side while springing on one foot.

HORIZONTAL PUNCH - A type of punch which, when delivered straight ahead, commences with the palm facing up, but concludes with the palm facing down (horizontally) upon contact. See CORKSCREW PUNCH.

HORIZONTAL ZONES - Another one of the categorical ZONES OF PROTECTION. It basically entails the protection of three horizontal or height levels: solar plexus to the top of the head, groin to the solar plexus and feet to the groin. Also known as HEIGHT ZONES.

HORIZONTAL ZONES OF ATTACK - It basically entails the striking to the three horizontal or height levels: solar plexus to the top of the head, groin to the solar plexus, and feet to the groin.

HORIZONTAL ZONES OF DEFENSE - Same as HORIZONTAL ZONES.

HORIZONTAL ZONES OF PROTECTION - Same as HORIZONTAL ZONES.

HORSE SENSE - A slang term for common sense. See COMMON SENSE.

HORSE STANCE - A training stance where the feet are slightly wider than the width of the shoulders. When settling in the stance the toes are turned in, heels forced out, back kept erect, and the knees bent and forced out. It is from this stance that all other stances evolve.

HUG(S) - To hold and press tightly.

HUGGING CHECK - Keeping close to and pressing up against a key area or areas on an opponent's body to minimize the leverage of his action.

HURT - To render pain or injury. See HARM.

HWRANG DO - A Korean Martial Art system that teaches high principles and philosophies. In addition to self-defense disciplines, advocates are dedicated to the cultivation of spirit and health among the youth.

HYBRID MOVES - Refined moves that require sophistication when implemented. These are the shorthand moves of Kenpo. See explanation of SHORTHAND MOVES.

HYPER EXTEND - To extend beyond the normal conditions.

I

IDEAL PHASE - This is PHASE I of the analytical process of dissecting a technique. It requires structuring an IDEAL technique by selecting a combat situation that you wish to analyze. Contained within the technique should be fixed moves of defense, offense, and the anticipated reactions that can stem from them. This PHASE strongly urges the need to analyze techniques from THREE POINTS OF VIEW. Refer to THREE POINTS OF VIEW, as well as FIRST, SECOND, and THIRD POINT OF VIEW.

IDEAS - One of the philosophical views of Kenpo that considers defensive and offensive moves to be no more than concepts that vary with each and every situation.

I.K.K.A. - The International Kenpo Karate Association originated in 1956 as the Kenpo Karate Association of America. It was registered with the State of California for the purposes of governing Kenpo in the continental U.S. The K.K.A.A. was changed to the I.K.K.A. in 1960 when association members began migrating to foreign countries.

IMPACT ADJUSTMENT - The ability to readjust your balance at the time of impact or contact. Consideration must also be given to the proper use of body alignment so as to decrease the possibility of injury when contact is made. The term is also related to BALANCE COMPENSATION.

IMPLOSIVE ACTION - Energy and power imploding from inside out.

INHALE - The intake of air during the breathing process.

INNER - Refers to principles that facilitate the development of the mind.

IN-PLACE - Remaining on the same spot.

IN-PLACE STANCE CHANGE - Changing from one stance to another while basically remaining on the same spot.

IN-PLACE TRANSITION - The transferring from one stance to another, or body position to another, while affixed to the same spot.

INSERT - The addition of a weapon or move, simultaneous with, or sandwiched between your base moves. Inserting is part of the EQUATION FORMULA, and is divided into two studies: (1) filling of dead space (SEQUENTIAL FLOW), and (2) its usefulness as a check or strike.

INSIDE DOWNWARD BLOCK - A particular method of blocking below your waist that requires your blocking arm to travel from outside, in. May be executed either palm up or palm down.

INSTRUCTOR - One who is in charge of, and qualified to teach, students.

INSURANCE - the use of checks, and all other means of protection to prevent your opponent from retaliating.

IN SYNC - precise unification of mind, breath, and physical forces which when brought into focus, maximizes your efforts.

INTEGRATION OF FORCES - The unification of power sources, which may or may not involve identical principles, that act in sync with each other in order to maximize the move rendered.

INTELLECTUAL - A term used in naming some of the self-defense techniques.

INTELLECTUAL MOVES - Moves that are guided by instinct rather than emotion and experience.

INTENTIONAL MOVES - Execution of planned moves.

INTERCEPT - To stop the opponent's action before it reaches its destination.

INTERCEPTING FORCES - A point in time and space, during your defensive or offensive action, where the force of your action merges with that of your opponent's action or reaction, to redirect or stop it.

INTERNALIZE - Moves that are so ingrained, that they can be activated instinctively. See NEURO MUSCULAR MEMORY, SPONTANEOUS STAGE, and INSTINCTIVE.

INTERNAL ORGANS - Refers to interrelated parts of the human body that function together to maintain life. These diverse organs include the heart, lungs, spleen, brain, kidneys, liver, etc.

INTERNAL SYSTEMS - This second school of thought believes that power, through proper breathing, can come from total relaxation. Breathing is slower and deeper. Evidence of special breathing is not apparent to your opponent. When an attack is launched, the stored air causes the body to explode into action. The expulsion of air is short and concise, and only upon contact does the body settle, tense, and brace to enhance the effectiveness of the strike. At the precise moment of contact, all forces — mind, breath, and strength — merge. See EXTERNAL SYSTEMS.

INTERNALIZE - Moves that are so ingrained that they can be activated instinctively.

INTERRUPTED FLOW - Any action, planned or otherwise, that disrupts the flow of a technique sequence. This interference can be caused by: (1) your opponent; or (2) by you, via the use of broken rhythm. Broken rhythm is no more than premeditated stuttering of motion used to baffle your opponent.

INTERSECTING ACTION - A point in time and space, where your and your opponent's action converge.

INTERSECTING FORCES - A critical point in time and space where all the forces of your action, stemming from various angles, merge and unite as one. The unification of all of these forces helps to insure KI or CHI. The converging of power sources. See CONVERGING FORCES and COLLIDING FORCES.

INTONATION OF MOTION - The manner of applying the final strike to a technique sequence.

INTUITIVE - The ability to perceive knowledge without the conscious use of reasoning.

INTUITIVE AWARENESS - The sense of feeling the presence of someone or something without seeing, touching, or hearing.

INWARD PARRY - A blocking method that requires your blocking arm to travel from outside to inside, as it redirects a blow or kick, by riding or going with the force.

IRON - Tournament slang for trophies.

J

JAMMER - One who constantly crowds his attacker. (Tournament slang.)

JAM(MING) - A special method of blocking that crowds or forces an opponent's natural weapon back and against its pivotal joint to prevent it from moving or functioning. JAMMING can also be accomplished by forcing an opponent's limb against other parts of his anatomy.

JERK(ING) - An explosive short and abrupt pull, push, or twist.

JET LAG - A term used in Kenpo to describe all moves that do not stem from their POINT OF ORIGIN. Time lags result from such actions, and restrict spontaneous responses. See POINT OF ORIGIN.

JIU-JITSU - An oriental form of wrestling known as the "body art". It involves the use of twisting, spraining, dislocating, breaking, and other like means against the joints and pressure points of the body. Throwing is also an integral part of the Art.

JOUSTING - A method of employing a natural weapon by placing it in a fixed position prior to having the body propel it.

JUDO - A more gentle form of oriental wrestling. Referred to as the "gentle way", it employs grabs, hip and shoulder throws, in addition to arm or leg locks and holds in its application.

JUMP - A method of maneuvering which involves moving forward, backward, or sideways by vigorously springing or leaping to avoid, or execute an attack.

KAJUKENBO - An offshoot of William Chow's original methods of Kenpo Karate that was created by Adriano and Joe Emperado of Hawaii. When dissecting the term KAJUKENBO, KA stands for Karate, JU for JiuJitsu and Judo, KEN for Kenpo, and BO for Chinese Boxing.

KARATE - A recent term used by the Japanese to describe the oriental boxing systems of Japan and Okinawa.

KATA - A Japanese term for the word FORM. See the definition for FORM.

KENPO - A modern term describing one of the more innovative systems of the Martial Arts which originally started in Hawaii, is heavily practiced in the Americas, and has now spread worldwide. KEN means fist, and PO means law. Because of Ed Parker's numerous contributions of innovative concepts and principles, many Kenpo practitioners are referring to modern day KENPO as PARKER KENPO.

KENPO CREST - Logo designed by Ed Parker and brother David for the American Kenpo System. All parts of the design have significant meaning, and symbolically represent the past and present. The following is a brief explanation of what the crest symbolizes:

(1) **THE TIGER** - represents earthly strength derived during the early stages of learning;

(2) **THE DRAGON** - represents spiritual strength, which comes with seasoning;

(3) **THE CIRCLE** - symbolic of (a) life itself, which is a continuous cycle without beginning or end, (b) all moves that evolve from a circle, whether they are defensive or offensive, (c) the bond of friendship that should continuously exist among system members, and (d) the base from which our alphabet stems;

(4) **THE DIVIDING LINES** - in the circle represent, (a) the original eighteen hand movements — directions in which the hands can travel, (b) angles from which an opponent or you can attack or defend, and (c) the pattern(s) in which the feet can travel;

(5) **THE COLORS** - represent proficiency, achievement and authority;

(6) **THE ORIENTAL WRITING** - is a reminder of the originators of our Art — the Chinese, and represents respect, but not subservience to them;

(7) **THE SHAPE** - (a) the TOP of the crest is like a roof, which gives shelter to all who are under it, (b) the SIDES are concave because, like the roof of a Chinese home, it will send evil back to from where it came, whenever it tries to enter, (c) the BOTTOM forms the shape of an ax — it represents the executioner — which cuts off members who shame or oppose the code(s) of the system.

KENPO KARATE - Term used by William Chow to describe the art he was teaching in Hawaii during the period of Ed Parker's training.

KEN TO - Is the Japanese term for boxing. KEN means fist, and TO means fight. Thus, Ken To means fist fight.

KI - The Japanese term for CHI (refer to CHI), where all power sources unify — the mind, body, spirit — all working together in perfect "sync".

KIAI - Loud noise caused by the rapid expulsion of air from the lower abdomen. The expulsion of air creates stability, increases force, fortifies the body, and can have a psychological effect upon your opponent. Kiai originally meant "breathing exercise".

KICK(S) - Generally refers to method(s) used when striking with the foot. It also includes striking with the shin, calf, peroneus longus, knee, or other parts of the leg.

KICKING SET I - A set required for Orange Belt that employs the ball kick, side kick, front and rear leg roundhouse kicks, rear kick, and spinning rear kick.

KICKING SET II - A set required for Second Degree Brown Belt that employs the front and rear leg chicken kicks, front and rear leg rear chicken kicks, thrusting sweep kicks, side chicken kicks, front and rear scoop kicks, spinning reverse heel scoop kicks, ball kicks, roundhouse kicks, side kicks, and rear kicks.

KILL OR BE KILLED - A method of combat learned by the military during World War II. It was a condensed form of combat utilizing Martial Art concepts, and concentrating on techniques that brought about instant disability or death.

KIMONO - Term used in self-defense techniques that symbolizes the lapel of a coat.

KINEMATICS - The analysis of an individual's physical structure and his personal bio-mechanical approach to a skill problem. See TAILORING.

KINESIOLOGY - The study of the principles of mechanics and anatomy in relation to human movement.

KINETICS - The science that deals with the motion of masses in relation to the forces acting on them. The analysis of a specific skill, and the effects of force, mass, and energy on the motions involved in that skill.

KNIFE - A bladed weapon made by man that can cut, pierce, slash, or stab.

KNIFE-EDGE - The outside flat edge of the hand or foot used as a natural weapon.

KNOCKOUT - A term used to describe an individual struck to an unconscious state. It is also a term used in some of the Professional Karate Tournaments in which competitors are allowed to literally knock their opponents out.

KNOWING WHERE TO HIT - Having knowledge of which targets to strike, and the order to strike them in, to render the greatest results for the least amount of effort.

KWOON - A Chinese term for school or training hall.

L

"L" SHAPED PATTERN - Pattern that is followed when doing SHORT FORM I.

LAGGING HAND - Hand that lags in its delivery. A hand that drags back before delivery.

LANCE - A term used in self-defense techniques when referring to a knife attack.

LATERAL MOMENTUM - Body momentum that originates from the side, and not only enhances power, but provides protection as well. The technique SNAPPING TWIG is a good example of LATERAL MOMENTUM. This is rotational force that employs the dimension of width.

LAUNCHING - (1) A type of CONTOURING requiring body contact, where the surface of your or your opponent's body is used to ricochet, leverage, or bounce from prior to traveling to your primary target. Such action helps to accelerate and, therefore, enhance the effectiveness of your strike. As an example, you can have an INWARD BLOCK ricochet into a HANDSWORD to the neck. Your defensive action was used to LAUNCH into an offensive one. (2) Use of a wall or floor to push off from to enhance, support, and brace the delivery of your strikes.

LAUNCHING EFFECT - Any action that uses one surface to ricochet, bounce or push off from in order to enhance, support, and brace the delivery of that action.

LAYMEN - Beginners in the Martial Arts.

LEAP - A type of springing jump used to evade or attack an opponent.

LEAVES - A term used in self-defense techniques when referring to the fingers.

LEFT SIDE COVER - This half cover takes place by shifting the right foot to the right as you turn counterclockwise and face the left flank. Whether facing 12 o'clock in a right or left neutral bow, it is only the right foot that steps to the right as you turn and face to the left. See SIDE COVER.

LEFT TO LEFT - A fighting position where both combatants face each other with their left foot forward.

LEFT TO RIGHT - A fighting position where your left foot is forward while your opponent leads with his right foot.

LEOPARD PUNCH - Same as a half fist. See HALF FIST.

LEVERAGE POINTS - Fixed points which, when force or pressure is applied, can either be used to throw an opponent or prevent him from taking action.

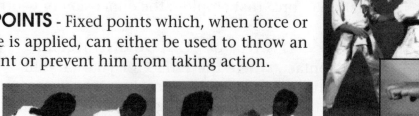

LEVERAGING - Term used to describe one of the methods of CONTOURING where the body of your opponent is used as a fulcrum, and your limbs are used as a lever to enhance the effectiveness of your action. Another related term is FULCRUMING.

LIFTING - The raising of an opponent to immobilize him, or that stage of action used prior to throwing him to the ground.

LIGAMENTS - Bands of tissue which attach bone to bone at the joints.

LIGHT CONTACT - Usually occurs in Amateur Karate Tournaments where competitors are not allowed to make heavy contact, and only light contact is allowed. Infraction of these rules can mean disqualification from the match and/or tournament, or points being awarded to the opponent. This is the type of contact allowed at the International Karate Championships held annually in Long Beach, California.

LIMITED RETALIATION - Inability to counter an opponent effectively because of encumbrances or unfavorable circumstances.

LINEAR MOVES - Movements that are direct in nature. Moves that specifically follow a straight line or path. Although these moves are primarily offensive, they can be used defensively. They are useful follow ups that often trail circular moves that meet resistance.

LINE OF ATTACK - Path that an opponent follows when attacking you. This LINE OF ATTACK can come from 12 o'clock, 4 o'clock, 8 o'clock, or from other numbers on the clock.

LINE OF DEPARTURE - The line, angle, or direction combatants can move to when escaping that will place them in a secure position.

LINE OF ENTRY - That line or path of penetration that allows you or your opponent access to targets via vertical ascension or descent. The weapon may be executed vertically, upward or downward, depending on whether you or your opponent are standing or in a prone position. To thwart your opponent's efforts you may (depending on your lead leg and how it is matched with that of your opponent's lead leg) be (1) on the line of entry, (2) on top of the line of entry (on top of your opponent's foot), (3) inside of the line of entry, and (4) over the line of entry. In contrast to the ANGLE OF ENTRY, the LINE OF ENTRY demands a specific path and direction of entry.

LINE OF SIGHT - (1) The path of a moving target brought into alignment. (2) The direction one faces when forming a stance. This direction is considered to be 12 o'clock when commencing a self-defense technique.

LINE RIDER - One who purposely and continuously steps out of bounds during a match. (Tournament slang.)

LOCALIZED SANDWICH - Strikes that are directly opposite each other when making contact with the target.

LOCK OUT - It is a type of check that is used to briefly detain the action of your opponent. It involves striking a target with a natural weapon, and having the weapon remain on the target for a time before retrieving it.

LOCK-OUT POWER - The concept that force and penetration can be increased by moves that fully extend and lock-out at the time of impact. This type of action also acts as a Time Deterrent, and temporarily stops an opponent from regaining his Point of Origin.

LOCKS - Moves that immobilize the joints or other body parts of your opponent, and restrain him from taking further action. They combine methods of pushing, pulling, and grabbing.

LONG FORM I - A form required for Orange Belt.

LONG FORM II - A form required for Blue Belt.

LONG FORM III - A form required for Third Brown Belt.

LONG RANGE ENCOUNTERS - Action that occurs at arms or legs length.

LONG RANGE WEAPONS - Refers to natural weapons that employ full extension in their execution.

LOOPING - A specialized method of employing a natural weapon that follows a circular path, either vertically or horizontally, commencing at the front, then to the side, and finally concluding over the head. A good example is the "looping back knuckle strike".

LOWER CASE MOVEMENT - Move that employs, among others, the SQUEEGEE PRINCIPLE, GEOMETRIC PATH, REVERSE MOTION, and ECONOMY OF MOTION. Here, another portion (lower) of the initial blocking or striking arm or leg is used in a combination, either defensively or offensively, because of potentially superior ANGLE OF ENTRY, ANGLE OF CONTACT, ANGLE OF INCIDENCE, ANGLE OF DISTURBANCE, or closer proximity to the next target or weapon. See UPPER CASE MOVEMENT.

M

MACE - A term used in self-defense techniques when referring to the fist.

MAGNETIC FIELD - Confining your movements within the aura of your body. Refer to the term FORCE FIELD.

MAGNIFIED DAMAGE - Injury that is intensified because of the highly technical use of principles.

MAINTAIN - (1) To sustain, for a length of time, whatever you are doing at the time. (2) A command during promotion where a student who has passed his test is asked to maintain his breath to lessen the effect of the kick he will receive as part of the ceremony.

MAINTAIN THE GAP - The strategic use of foot maneuvers, as well as body maneuvers, to continually keep at a safe distance from your opponent.

MAJOR AREAS - The major weak points of the body; solar plexus, throat, kidneys, eyes, knees, etc. VITAL AREAS where damage can be most devastating. See VITAL AREAS and TARGETS.

MAJOR MOVES - Strong and positive moves which cause immediate devastation.

MANEUVERS - Ways you can move your feet, arms or body to initiate or avoid an attack. Methods used to close or extend your range.

MANNER OF ENTRY - The method(s) used to approach a target.

MAN-MADE WEAPONS - All weapons made by man, excluding his natural weapons (fists, elbows, knees, feet, etc.).

MARGIN FOR ERROR - The execution of a defensive and/or offensive move which, when delivered, gives you greater latitude to work with in the event of error or miscalculation.

MARRIAGE OF GRAVITY - Same as GRAVITATIONAL MARRIAGE. Both terms are used interchangeably.

MARTIAL ARTIST - An individual who is an actual practitioner of the Martial Arts.

MARTIAL ARTS - Term that is generally used to describe the self-defense systems of the Orient.

MASTER KEY BASIC - A single move that can be used in more than one predicament with equal effect.

MASTER KEY MOVEMENT(S) - A move or series of moves that can be used in more than one predicament. For example, a rear heel kick, shin scrape, and instep stomp can be used for a FULL NELSON, REAR BEAR HUG with the arms free or pinned, REAR ARM LOCK, etc. Similarly, an arm break can be applied to a cross wrist grab, a lapel grab, or hair grab - application of the arm break would remain constant, but the methods of controlling the wrist would vary.

MASTER KEY TECHNIQUES - The sequence of movements that can be applied to a number of predicaments. See FAMILY RELATED MOVES.

MATCHING COUNTER - Applying what your opponent does — scissors on scissors, pin on pin, grab on grab, etc. It is the matching of the same action applied by your opponent to deter his action or cause him pain.

MATHEMATICAL AND GEOMETRICAL SYMBOL CONCEPTS - There are three mathematic symbols; the minus, plus, and times sign and three geometric symbols; the square, triangle, and circle, that can enhance student learning. This concept, can be paralleled with the CLOCK PRINCIPLE, provides similar results, and with them a better understanding of DIRECTION and PATHS OF TRAVEL.

MATTER AND MOTION - The concept that while matter comes in such forms as solids, liquids and gases, motion (physical moves) can also be applied in a solid, liquid, and gaseous state.

MEANINGFUL DIALOGUE - An adopted term that denotes applying contact of some significance when working opposite one another. Although contact penetration is somewhat controlled, and no injuries have been sustained, the recipient of such action knows he has been hit.

MECHANICAL - Refers to those whose movements are very staccato in execution and appearance. Sequence of movements which look as if it is being done by-the-numbers. Movements are robot-like in appearance.

MECHANICAL STAGE - That stage of learning where movements are clarified and defined, and thus, given meaning and purpose. Movements at this stage, however, are applied mechanically, and a student is more equipped to verbalize answers than to utilize them physically.

MECHANIC OF MOTION - A practitioner whose knowledge is such that he can analyze, dissect, and assemble techniques. With this ability he not only gains a greater understanding of their principles and counterparts, but can teach as well.

MEDITATION - A brief period of mental relaxation used in Kenpo to eliminate outside distractions. Once this is accomplished, the student can more fully concentrate on the activities that are to be learned in class. Taking the time to do this helps to avoid unnecessary injuries which might otherwise occur.

MEDIUM RANGE WEAPON - A natural weapon that extends no more than half the distance of a fully extended strike. In some instances, it may refer to using the midway point of a LONG RANGE WEAPON to obtain this desired range. Its use requires total knowledge of principles for it to be effective. Properly applied, it can be devastating during critical, but opportune moments of exposure. If you lack knowledge of its use, then the opportunities to take advantage of timely exposures diminish.

MEET - Refers to having your movements merge with your opponent's action at a strategic distance from you.

MENTAL DISTRACTION - Use of deliberate methods to force an opponent to place his concern and efforts elsewhere so that the real target objective is defenseless. Application of pressure, FEINTING, distorted facial expressions, and yelling are forms of mental distraction.

MENTAL HARMONY - All functions of the body in total unison with the mind.

MENTAL SPEED - Mental speed is the quickness of the mind to select the appropriate movements to effectively deal with the perceived combat situation. Speed of this type can only be increased by practicing on a regular basis.

METHOD(S) OF DISTURBANCE - Tactics you can employ to upset, confuse, confound, or trouble an opponent.

METHOD(S) OF EXECUTION - The manner in which a move is executed to insure maximum results. Such moves can follow a direct, dipping, looping, hooking, or roundhouse path.

MID-POINT BALANCE - The striking of body limbs in various (including opposite) directions while the center of your body mass remains stationary and balanced. This center, or mid-point of your body mass, although fixed and stable, does nothing to detract from or enhance the effects of your multiple strikes. Therein lies the value of its use.

MID-WAY POINT - It is that location or refuge point that places you equidistant from two assailants previously encountered.

MIND OVERLOAD - Trying to comprehend too much at one time. Instead of absorbing and retaining information, the mind gets cluttered with information, and ends up remembering less.

MINOR/MAJOR PRINCIPLE - The principle that a minor move, while it is subordinate and not devastating in itself, can cause ample damage and/or delay to allow the execution of a major move to occur. Major moves are strong and positive moves which cause immediate devastation.

MINOR MOVE(S) - Subordinate moves which are frequently prefixes, suffixes, or inserts that are often necessary ingredients in the set up and execution of major moves.

MIRROR IMAGE/REVERSE - The opposite of whatever you employ. For example, the mirror image of a right outward block is a left outward block.

MIRROR PRINCIPLE - The matching of stances, positions, postures, blocks, strikes, etc. from the standpoint of a MIRROR IMAGE. MIRROR IMAGES automatically display the opposite side of what you should look like. It can be said that the terms MIRROR IMAGE and OPPOSITE are synonymous.

MIS-COMMUNICATION - (1) The misinterpretation of an opponent's true intentions. (2) Planned moves and gestures that are purposely used to mislead an opponent.

MOMENTARY CONDITIONING - The ability to condition an opponent to accept one thing, then surprising him by unexpectedly switching your strategy. Changes in your actions then allow easy access to other vulnerable targets as a result of his conditioned reaction.

MOMENTARY LEVITATION - A brief moment of suspension in air prior to using marriage of gravity when kicking or striking. An example of this can be found in the self-defense technique called the LEAP OF DEATH.

MOMENTARY PREVENTION - Slight detention of your opponent's actions and/or reactions to avoid a counter that may be intentional, or otherwise.

MONITORING - The ability to observe your opponent's fighting mannerisms during the course of combat, decipher his actions, and instinctively employ effective counters to his actions.

MOTHER/FATHER MOVES - In Kenpo we can think of the initial defensive positioning of your arms as father/mother movements. A left inward block would be a father movement, and the positioning of your right arm would be the mother movement (right arm hanging naturally at your side, cocked at the hip, cocked at the ear, etc.). It is the initial move that protects you. Just as your parents come first, so do the protective blocks. Thus, a technique such as Dance of Death has a left inward block as its father and the naturally hanging right arm is its mother. Likewise, Flashing Wings uses a left inward block as its father, and the cocked right arm at the hip as its mother. The technique, Five Swords utilizes a right inward block as its father movement and the left checking hand as its mother movement.

MOTION ANALYSIS - Examination of each of the component parts of the Martial Arts and how these many elements of motion interrelated.

MOVE - (1) A command used when teaching to cause a student to react during a particular exercise. (2) The traveling of any object from one point to another.

MOVEMENTS OF PUNCTUATION - Moves that can be randomly or intermittently inserted within a prescribed technique sequence without disrupting its flow of action. They are in-between moves (MINOR MOVES) that are used as additives to enhance the effect and flow of motion. It is synonymous with the terms COMPOUNDING A TECHNIQUE and HIDDEN MOVES.

MOVING UP THE CIRCLE - Refers to having the rear leg of a neutral bow stance circle clockwise or counter clockwise in order to give reach to the arm that's doing the striking. See SHORTENING THE CIRCLE.

MULTIPLE APPLICATION - The utilization of more than one weapon employed simultaneously, consecutively, or intermittently.

MULTIPLE ATTACK - An attack by two or more opponents.

MUMBLING MOTION - Movements that are not executed with crispness. They can be compared with words that lack diction or are slurred when spoken. See SCRIBBLING.

MUSCLE TONE - That state in which some of the fibers of a muscle are in constant contraction, thus giving it a quality of firmness.

MUSCLING - Generally refers to the application of force minus the use of skill and strategy. To execute moves with force while lacking the knowledge of principles necessary for proper application and maximum results.

MUSCULAR BRACE - Refers to following the sophisticated principles of kinesiology, where we must learn to position our muscles to act as a brace or support when meeting resistance. All of this is done in anticipation of the impact that is to occur. It is related to IMPACT ADJUSTMENT and BALANCE COMPENSATION. See BRACING ANGLE.

MUSCULAR SYSTEMS - An assemblage of fiber cells that can contract or expand upon signal from the nervous system to produce body movements.

N

NATURAL DEFENSES - The use of body parts as defensive blocks or deterrents.

NATURAL MOTION - Moves that are native to the body, and that are inherent when activated. Unnatural moves, through practice, can also become natural.

NATURAL VS POSITIONAL - Natural refers to the normal state of the body, where the torso and limbs are relaxed and unaffected in terms of posture. Positional indicates that the body posture takes on an intentional, controlled pose or attitude.

NATURAL WEAPONS - The use of body parts as offensive weapons. This includes using parts of the hand, arm, foot, leg, head, etc.

NEEDLING - A method of CONTOURING that requires two natural weapons to simultaneously TRACK their way to their targets.

NEURO MUSCULAR MEMORY - The body's ability to function without thought. See INSTINCTIVE, INTERNALIZE, and SPONTANEOUS STAGE.

NEUTRAL BOW - This stance allows for greater mobility than the FORWARD BOW in terms of retreating or advancing with ease. The width of this stance is formed by having one foot ahead of the other, utilizing the Toe/Heel relationship, that is the toe of the forward foot should be in line with the heel of the rear foot on a 180 degree line intersecting your opponent's vertical axis. The depth of this stance is formed by a Heel/Knee relationship, that is the heel of the forward foot should be in line with the knee of the rear leg when it is smartly and naturally placed on the ground. Both feet should run parallel to each other at an angle of 45 degrees from your opponent. Your weight should be evenly distributed (50/50), with your knees slightly bent. See FORWARD BOW.

NEUTRALIZED HANDS - The placing of your hand(s) in a neutral position from which it (they) can readily nullify an attack, initiate an attack, or trigger a counter attack.

NEUTRALIZING - Methods used to check, as well as nullify an opponent's action for a brief time period. These methods may employ PINNING, PRESSING, JAMMING, HUGGING, POSITIONAL CHECKS, BUCKLING, etc. It may also include methods used to alter postural positions that momentarily disallows an opponent from retaliating. The latter methods effectively control, height, width, and depth zones of an opponent. This term is not the same as NEUTRALIZED HANDS.

NEUTRAL ZONES OF DEFENSE (PROTECTION) - These areas are literally zones where one can find momentary sanctuary. They are synonymously referred to as zones of sanctuary. These zones can be found in the corners of a square that engulfs a circle. (See illustrations.) The theory works on the premise that when an opponent attacks you using a circular motion (delivered vertically, diagonally, or horizontally) you are to take sanctuary in the corners of an imaginary square where the zones are neutral because circular moves cannot make contact with the corners of the square that engulfs it.

NO CONTACT - The ability to execute a strike with control so that no contact is made with the designated target. This rule is adhered to at some of the Amateur Karate Tournaments.

NO CONTROL - Lack of restraint. Inability to restrain offensive moves from causing injury.

NONSENSE - Absurdity and foolishness. Lack of common sense.

NONSENSICAL MOVES - Absurd use of motion that lacks logic and wisdom when applied.

NORMAL FLOW - Sequence of movements that pursue unaltered rhythm.

NORTHERN STYLES - Generally refers to those Martial Art systems practiced in Northern China. These systems place great emphasis on kicking, rolling on the floor, and strenuous acrobatic feats.

NUDGING - Specialized move describing a light push.

NULLIFY - The prevention of an opponent's intentional or unintentional moves.

NUNCHAKU - A weapon used by the Okinawans to overcome their Japanese oppressors. The weapon itself consists of two wooden handles that are attached by rope or chain. They were originally used to thrash rice stalks.

NUNCHAKU SET - Requirement for 2nd Degree Black.

OBJECT OBSCURITY - The use of one body limb to hide the action of another. For example, after a right two finger hook is applied to the left eye of your opponent, your left hand can then use your right forearm as a track to zero in on the same target. Not until the left two finger poke is almost on target do you retract your right arm. The last minute replacement of weapons makes the second action obscure. This concept parallels the principle of TRACKING and is classified as being a method of CONTOURING.

OBJECTS TO TARGETS - The use of free, loose, or immovable objects found in our environment in place of our natural weapons to strike targets on an opponent.

OBSCURE ZONES - Those areas of space that are outside of the boundaries of our peripheral vision. These zones of space are BLIND SPOTS from which action can originate, and be delivered unchecked. Movements involving the penetration of OBSCURE ZONES are more often than not calculated movements utilizing deceptive angles. Footwork becomes increasingly important when penetrating these zones, especially when the related DEPTH ZONES affect your critical distance. This term is also known as ZONES OF OBSCURITY.

OBVIOUS CARRIES - A method in which one could carry a Nunchaku unconcealed in his belt or pants. Its exposure makes it evident, and therefore, a possible deterrent.

OFFENSE - Offensive moves employed against an opponent to score points (tournament), or to injure or defeat (self-defense).

OFFENSIVE CHECK - A single move which first acts as a check before becoming a strike or hit. See DETAINING CHECK. ▶

OFFSET - An assailant who is not standing directly in front of or opposite you prior to, during, or after a confrontation. When standing and facing you, your assailant's right shoulder is opposite your right shoulder or vice versa.

ONE-LEG STANCE - Commonly used while jumping from one side to avoid a front or rear attack. The supporting leg determines a right or left One Leg Stance.

OPEN END TRIANGLE - Refers to the positioning of your body parts so that they form a triangle that has an open end. Use of these body formations help to funnel, wedge, trap, or prevent an opponent from injuring you.

OPEN(ING) THE GAP - To increase the distance between you and your opponent for whatever strategic purpose desired.

OPPOSING FORCES - The directing of two convergent moving forces so that when collision occurs the impact is greatly increased. If strategically planned and calculated you can use your force in opposition to your opponent's force to defeat him. This is known as borrowed force, that is, it is you who are purposefully borrowing your opponent's force to add to the force of your own strike.

OPPOSITE - The other side or MIRROR IMAGE of whatever you execute. See MIRROR IMAGE.

OPPOSITE MOTION - The principle that any motion done to one side can be matched on the other side.

OPTIMUM ANGLE OF INCIDENCE - The best and most ideal angle of contact for a given situation or desired effect.

OPTIONS - The inherent natural defensive and offensive abilities and alternatives that work for you.

ORBITAL ADJUSTMENT - A slight degree change when altering the orbit of your action.

ORBITAL CHANGE - Use of the eight directions to orbit your action.

ORGANIZED RETROGRADE - Use of reverse motion that is contrary to the normal order.

OUT OF CONTACT - First stage of the FOUR STAGES OF RANGE. It refers to that stage of distance that places you out of the reach of your opponent or vice versa.

OUTER - Implies the learning of physical skills and physiological principles.

OUTER PERIMETER - That imaginary circle surrounding the head and feet that "offensive" moves should be confined to if you wish to render greater power and speed when executing such action. It is not to be confused with the OUTER RIM principle which requests that you not over-extend or over-commit your "defensive" moves.

OUTER RIM CONCEPT - An imaginary egg-shaped circle that is used as a visual aid. This egg-shaped pattern starts at eyebrow level, and ends slightly below the region of the groin. The larger portion of the egg is positioned at the top. This concept teaches you to confine defensive and offensive movements of your arms and hands to those areas within the imaginary circle. You learn never to over-extend nor over-commit beyond the circle with your arms and hands. To do so not only exposes your vital areas, but limits your ability to counter quickly. Employing this concept reduces the number of openings in your defense, and with them, the odds of getting hit. It is a supplemental aid in the study of the ZONE CONCEPT.

OUTSIDE DOWNWARD BLOCK - A type of block requiring your blocking arm to travel from inside out. It is used for attacks that are primarily directed to targets below the waist.

OUTWARD PARRY - A block that travels from inside out as it redirects and rides the force of your opponent's action.

OVER-REACH - To over-extend oneself with a blow or kick needlessly, or to reach beyond or above a certain point unnecessarily. Target exposure is the result of such action.

OVER-ROTATE - The use of excessive body torque, where torquing beyond a certain point begins to detract from obtaining maximum force. Beyond this point Directional Harmony is violated, and Disharmony of Direction occurs. "To split your direction is to split your force." See POINT OF OVERTURN.

P

PACING - The regulation of rhythmic timing.

PARAGRAPH OF MOTION - Series of defensive and offensive moves that are used consecutively, on one or more opponents, without an interruption in the flow of action.

PARANORMAL PERCEPTION - Refers to intuitive awareness; the ability to sense the presence of entities or things without smelling, seeing or hearing them; or an ability to predict occurrences before they happen.

PARASYMPATHETIC - This term is associated with the autonomic nervous system which has a part in increasing the tone and contractility of smooth muscle and dilation of blood vessels.

PARRY - Redirecting a blow or kick by riding or going with the force.

PARRYING BLOCK - Blocking moves that redirect, ride, and go with the force of your opponent's action.

PARTIAL ARTISTS - A slang term describing those martial artists whose system is very limited in knowledge, substance, and material, but who profess to be superior over all others.

PASSIVE KI OR CHI - The harmonious unification of the conscious and subconscious minds to achieve masterful creations of the mind. Synchronized breathing with physical movement (other than the minor dexterity needed to complete their work) is not necessary to obtain Passive Ki or Chi. It is the mind alone that climaxes and transcends. This method of achieving power is predominant among scholars, intellects, inventors, and engineers.

PATH - See GEOMETRIC PATH.

PATH OF EXECUTION - Although, technically, both PATH OF EXECUTION and PATH OF TRAVEL can be used interchangeably, PATH OF EXECUTION more specifically refers to the route that an offensive move follows when traveling to its target. It can be delivered horizontally, vertically, or diagonally.

PATH OF TRAVEL - This term generally refers to the route that a defensive move follows when traveling to its point of contact. It also can be delivered horizontally, vertically, or diagonally. Here again, technically, both PATH OF TRAVEL and PATH OF EXECUTION can be used interchangeably.

PATTERN ADDICT - One who is caught up in traditionally prescribed movements.

PEACH - A term used in self-defense techniques to refer to the testicles.

PENDULUM - A term used in self-defense techniques referring to a downward block or strike.

PENETRATION - This involves depth of focus. It is the extension of power beyond the selected target to insure the desired force and to compensate for the distance to be traveled.

PENETRATION POINT - An imaginary point that extends an inch or two beyond your selected target. Visualizing this point teaches you not to tense your arm or leg prematurely when punching, kicking, striking, etc. Following this principle will not only enhance your speed, but will proportionately add power as well.

PERCEPTUAL SPEED - Refers to the quickness with which the senses monitor the stimuli that they receive, determine the meaning of that stimuli, and the degree of speed with which the perceived information is conveyed to the brain so that MENTAL SPEED can parlay a response.

PERIPHERAL ASSESSMENT - The ability to observe and evaluate all surroundings without concentrating on any one specific area.

PERIPHERAL AWARENESS - The ability to visually interpret your surroundings prior to a confrontation. A visual means of registering what you see at all times so as to react in time to eliminate the threat. PERIPHERAL ASSESSMENT is part of PERIPHERAL AWARENESS. Also refer to MONITORING.

PERIPHERAL INTERPRETATION - Your logical summation and conclusion drawn from the environmental stimuli registered in your peripheral awareness.

PERIPHERAL REGISTERING - The recording of mental entries.

PERIPHERAL SCANNING - Viewing your environment or situation by taking fleeting glances.

PERIPHERAL VISION - The ability to see 180 degrees to both sides of the center of your body.

PERPETUAL CONTROL - Continuous control of an opponent's actions. The use of one hand to control while the other hand strikes, then switching so that control remains constant.

PHASE I - See IDEAL PHASE.

PHASE II - See WHAT IF PHASE.

PHASE III - See FORMULATION PHASE.

PHONETICS OF MOTION - Teaching a move or moves in progressive stages to get the maximum force from its execution. It is a method of teaching students movements BY-THE-NUMBERS.

PHYSICAL PREPAREDNESS - All phases of preventive planning to avoid, control, or win a physical encounter.

PHYSICAL SPEED - Refers to the promptness of physical movement (body performance) — the fluency in response to the perceived stimulus. It is the speed of the actual execution of a technique.

PIN - The pressing of joints or other key areas on an opponent's body with your own body to momentarily keep him confined and thus prevent him from taking action. A method used to CHECK the retaliatory efforts of an opponent. See PINNING CHECK.

PINCHER - An old self-defense technique formerly required for Yellow Belt.

PINCHING - The squeezing of various body parts of an opponent between your fingers and thumb, or other parts of your body, in order to cause pain or discomfort.

Pinch vs. Grab

PINNING BLOCK - A block which becomes a restraining, vice-like move to hinder an opponent from taking action.

PINNING CHECK - A restraining, vice like move to hinder an opponent from taking action.

PIN-POINT EFFECT - This is a principle that follows the effects of a pin, where the surface of the natural weapon being used is concentrated to as small an area as possible in order to have a more penetrating effect on the target. While surface injury is at a minimum the internal effects are much greater. Refer to SURFACE CONCENTRATION.

PIVOT - The changing from one stance or position to another while in place. This is done without moving the foot from the spot it is in.

PIVOTING - Another method of CONTOURING, where the contour of the body is used as a fulcrum to leverage and aid the effect of your action. PIVOTING can use the body as an axis. As an example, a heel palm strike to the chin can very easily be converted into a five finger slice by using the chin as the pivoting axis. The term WINDSHIELD WIPER is often used to describe this principle.

PIVOT POINT - That point, spot, position, level, etc. which various body parts use as an axis on which to turn.

PIVOTING AXIS - A stationary revolving point.

PLACEMENT OF TARGET - See TARGET PLACEMENT.

PLANE THEORY - This theory entails utilizing the principles involved in LAUNCHING a jet aircraft off of the deck of an aircraft carrier, and paralleling them with the execution of a punch. The fist is viewed as the aircraft, and the legs as the catapult. When harmoniously employed the two forces (punch and leg shuffle) not only maximize power, they allow the opposite hand to act as a check. Use of this principle triggers the BLACK DOT FOCUS concept. See CATAPULT(ING).

PLANNED REACTION - Premature response by an opponent caused by your predetermined movement or movements designed to distract or create an opening in his defenses.

PLANT - (1) To smartly place your foot (feet) on the ground. This can be done by raising and setting your foot (feet) from one spot to another. (2) This term is also a command used in class when learning basic foot manuevers.

PLEDGES - PLEDGES are extensions of the CREED, composed and designed to further promulgate spiritual character among the lower ranks.

PLUNGER THEORY - The idea that internal explosion associated with spontaneous action should not be paralleled to the detonation of dynamite via a plunger. Plungers react faster than a fuse, but they still require more time than that of an electronic detonator. See FUSE and ELECTRONIC DETONATOR THEORIES.

POINT OF ACTIVITY - Center of action where attention should be focused.

POINT OF CANCELLATION - Neutralizing point or position that nullifies a threat even if it is for a brief moment.

POINT OF CONTACT - Location of impact where weapon meets target.

POINT OF ORIGIN - The beginning, root, or source of any movement. The natural position or location of your body and natural weapon at the time action begins.

There is no "and" using point of origin

POINT OF REFERENCE - (1) That point of origin of a specific natural weapon, move, or technique sequence that one can refer to before proceeding to the next comparative stage, establishing other options, or duplicating it to the opposite side. (2) The selection of a basic move or technique sequence to fashion all others from. This concept is also called REFERENCE POINT.

POINT OF VIEW - See VIEWPOINT.

POKE - Refers to the thrusting of the tips or joints of the fingers to particular target areas on an opponent's body. The primary targets are the eyes.

POSITION - (1) A command used while teaching which has a student assume his original starting position. (2) A set or arranged posture used in class for training purposes other than mentioned, or when fighting. (3) How your or your opponent's body is angled.

POSITIONAL AIM - The specific alignment of a natural weapon prior to delivery. See POSITIONAL COCK.

POSITIONAL ALIGNMENT - Same as POSITIONAL AIM.

POSITIONAL OR POSITIONED CHECK - The for-mation of various defensive postures that automatically check incoming action. The structured positions themselves act as checks without any effort on your part. Refer to CHANGING OF THE GUARD.

POSITIONAL COCK - The placing of an intended block or strike in an ideal pose prior to delivering it.

POSITIONAL DEPTH OF ACTION - The specific angling, positioning, or placing of a limb to a selected depth so that the final position also acts as a buckle, or causes a sprain, break, or other like effects.

POSITIONS OF READINESS - These are positions that can be assumed prior to, during, or after combat. Having knowledge of these positions can greatly enhance your strategy by lessening the effects of your attacker, as well as assuring a more successful attack. They vary in hand and leg positions, depending upon the fighting experience of your opponent.

POSTURAL POSITIONS - Assumed body positions for the purpose of defense or offense.

POSTURE - The position of the body that is characteristic of a specific individual, or one that is assumed for purposes of defense or offense.

POWER - The ability to channel strength to achieve maximum force. Properly executed, it looks like force that is being expended without effort.

PRACTICAL MOVES - Realistic moves that are functional in combat. Moves that not only work during practice, but on the streets as well.

PRACTICAL KENPO - The use of the logical and realistic moves in the Kenpo system. They are not fancy, flowery, nor impractical.

PRACTICE - To engage in frequent workouts so that the increased number of repetitions proportionately adds to one's proficiency.

PRACTICE VS. TRAINING - PRACTICE is a rehearsed workout that instills routine habit. TRAINING is a disciplined workout that is performed more vigorously.

PRACTITIONER - One who learns, teaches, and practices the Martial Arts.

PRE-COMMITMENT - Purposeful moves that are preplanned, and utilized in setting an opponent up.

PREDETERMINED LABELING - Wrongfully believing a person to be what he really isn't, which can be a disadvantage when action occurs.

PREFIX - The addition of a weapon or move which precedes the BASE MOVE.

PREPARATORY CONSIDERATIONS - The initial planning of logical preventive measures to avoid danger, or eliminate a physical encounter from occurring.

PREPARATORY TORQUE - The rotational positioning of a selected body limb to make it ready in terms of increasing the torque of the next strike.

PRESENCE - The stateliness and poise of an individual who seems to exude power by just being there. Such poise distinguishes him from the "crowd", and often generates intimidation.

PRE-SET MOVEMENTS - Movements that are methodically planned prior to their use, and that generally work as conceived.

PRESSING - Application of a steady and continuous push.

PRESSING CHECKS - A contact method of CONTOURING, where the natural weapon is used to place pressure as it parallels the body surface of an opponent to keep him in check. Combinations of GRAVITATIONAL CHECKS and PRESSING CHECKS can be used simultaneously if desired.

PRESSURE POINTS - Vulnerable nerve points on the body that take little pressure to cause weakness, partial paralysis, or excruciating pain.

PRESSURE RELIEF - Applying of pressure to one area to allow relief to other pressure points.

PRE-STRETCH - A triggering of nerve receptors in your tendons to prepare the muscle for action. Example: "mini-warm-ups" such as cocking your leg prior to kicking. This increases the force of your delivery.

PREVENTIVE MOTION - (1) Movements that are used to ward off attacks, or (2) to stabilize or brace a target in order to increase the effectiveness of your strikes. These moves may be executed as parries, light blocks, or pushes against an opponent who is stationary, or who may be actively attacking.

PRIMITIVE - Embryonic state of movements. Moves that are singular in purpose. See EMBRYONIC BASICS.

PRIMITIVE STAGE - Early stage of development where moves are crudely executed.

PRINCIPLE - A comprehensive and fundamental rule stemming from a theory which, through devoted analysis, developed into the proven characteristics and facts that made it doctrine.

PRINCIPLE OF LIMITED RETALIATION - The use of CHECKS to prevent an opponent from taking immediate action. Methods used to detain the action(s) of an opponent.

PROGRESSIVE DIRECTIONAL HARMONY - Consistent use of all energies and forces traveling in the same direction, even after changing angles. Angle changes should not disrupt your continuance of principle.

PROLONGED EXPOSURE - The exposure of vital areas for too long a period that can result in being hit.

PRONE POSITIONS - Refers to lying flat or prostrate in a horizontal position, and face down.

PRONGS - A term used in self-defense techniques, to refer to the thumbs.

PRONOUNCE A MOVE - An analogy used so that a student realizes that basic moves are to be learned in stages, like the phonetic pronunciation of a word. This process is used only during training. After getting acquainted with the power derived from the ideal positions, one should then learn to use the basic moves realistically, without exaggeration or hesitation, and from their POINT OF ORIGIN.

PROPORTIONAL CONTOURING - Following whatever shape is presented at the time of action. The size and shape of individuals differ, and therefore, one must confine himself to following the contour of the shape at hand.

PROPORTIONAL EXECUTION - Moves designed for your particular body type so that when executed they strike with maximum efficiency.

PROPORTIONAL MOVEMENT - Same as PROPORTIONAL EXECUTION.

PROTECTION - All efforts employed that shield one from injury or devastation.

PROTECTIVE MEASURE - Back-up moves that lay in check, and that can be effectively used when called upon.

PROVISIONAL BLACK BELT - Same as APPRENTICE BLACK BELT.

PSYCHIC AWARENESS - Having knowledge of what will happen before it happens, and before there is any indication to others that it will happen.

PSYCHIC COMBAT AWARENESS - Ability to read what your opponent plans to do before he reveals it.

PSYCHIC REASSURANCE - Acquired and developed knowledge beyond the known physical processes, which comforts the mind, and instills confidence.

PSYCHOLOGICAL STRATEGY - The ability to employ one's attitude, demeanor, or conversation to thwart an impending crisis. It entails the use of brain rather than brawn in coping with physical encounters.

PULL DRAG - A type of FOOT MANEUVER that requires the supporting leg to pull rather than push when executing this particular method of SHUFFLING.

PULLING - (1) Bringing an object or person to you. (2) The ability to control a strike to within a fraction of an inch from hitting its target.

PUNCH - Primarily refers to the methods used when striking with the front portion of the fist.

PURPOSE OF ACTION - Any movement designed with a specific aim in mind, and which eludes inapplicable activity.

PURPOSEFUL COMPLIANCE - A deliberate portion of an opponent's offensive ac- hance your own action. When an oppo- you toward him during the course of a grab, force to increase the force of your counter

PURPOSEFUL DEFIANCE - (1) Deliberate resis- particular force of your opponent, to divert the attention of that opponent from the main counter you are preparing. (2) To use this resis- tance to activate a response from your opponent that can be used against him. This concept is found in the self-defense technique Obscure Sword, where your opponent's response is to pull you back toward him. It is at this moment that you borrow his force to enhance your strike.

PURSUANT AGGRESSION - Persistent and continued follow ups while attacking.

PUSH - To press against an opponent with steady force in order to drive him forward (away from you), downward, or outward without striking.

PUSH-DRAG - A type of SHUFFLE requiring your forward or rear leg to raise slightly before having the supporting leg push forward or back. The pushing leg must then drag toward the opposite leg so that the distance between them returns to its original depth. Once the original depth is re-established you are ready to resume the next PUSH-DRAG SHUFFLE. This is one of the four methods of SHUFFLING and one of three methods of obtaining BODY MOMEMTUM utilizing the dimension of DEPTH.

PUSHDOWN BLOCK - A particular blocking method that uses the heel of the palm to control the opponent's strike. It is normally directed to targets below the waist.

PUZZLE PRINCIPLE - The fitting of natural weapons to the target that they strike. It is one of the methods of CONTOURING. See FITTING.

QUADRANT ZONE CONCEPT - This concept is more concerned with defense and specific areas of the body that need to be protected rather than with those areas to be attacked. The theory divides each of the zones of height, width, and depth into two areas. A vertical imaginary rectangle is then superimposed over the height and width zones to create four quadrants (often referred to as gates). See illustration.

QUARTER BEAT TIMING - Use of one quarter timing to disturb the rhythmic patterns that may have already been established.

QUARTERING ZONES - Dividing any one of the zones into four parts. See QUADRANT ZONE CONCEPT.

QUICKNESS - Although this term normally refers to prompt reaction, Kenpo practitioners like to think of it as referring to the promptness of the mind, or the speed with which one can mentally observe and assess in order to promptly and properly react. See SPEED plus PERCEPTUAL, MENTAL, and PHYSICAL SPEED.

R

RAKE(ING) - The execution of a body weapon in a sweeping manner, so that it grazes the target with penetrating force. It involves increasing the depth of your circular path, so that your natural weapon gouges the surface of your target. It is similar to a SLICE, but with two exceptions — the force is greater, and the depth is more penetrating. Executed properly, a RAKE may employ several parts of a natural weapon, producing a corrugated effect when making contact with the target.

RAM - A term used in self-defense techniques, referring to a tackle.

RANGE - The distance which exists between you and your opponent.

REACTION - Response stemming from a stimulus or strike.

REACTIONARY ANTICIPATION - The contemplation of your action on an opponent, whereby causing a certain reaction on his part that will assist and increase the effectiveness of your follow-up action. This initial action not only improves angle of alignment, but assists you in borrowing your opponent's force as well.

REACTIONARY POSTURES AND POSITIONS - Postures and positions that result from being struck. Positions that often occur in response to pain.

REACTIONARY SET-UP - The ability to plan your action to cause your opponent to respond with a predictable reaction. Creating predictable reactions makes it easier to determine your next strike or defense. Having an opponent respond to the designs of your action helps to increase your opponent's vulnerability.

REAM - A special method used in knife fighting, where you twist the weapon after having thrust it.

REAR CROSSOVER - A type of foot maneuver which entails having the back foot cross over and in back of the forward leg, or the forward leg move over and in back of the rear leg when moving forward or backward.

REARRANGE - Shifting or changing the sequential order of movements. One of the key ingredients of the EQUATION FORMULA.

REBOUNDING CHECK - A check that occurs on the return of a blow or strike.

REBOUNDING STRIKE - Any strike that springs back after colliding with your or your opponent's body which then can be catapulted into a follow-up strike.

RECOIL - To spring back after a blow or kick has been delivered. Fast retrieve after delivery.

RECOILING CHECK - Same as REBOUNDING CHECK.

RECOVER - (1) To get well; (2) Another term used for the word "position", and meaning to return to your original starting position or point of origin.

REDIRECT - To alter the direction of an attacking weapon.

REFERENCE POINT - See POINT OF REFERENCE.

REFLEX TIME - The time between the beginning of a stimulus and the resulting action (usually 25 to 30 milliseconds).

REGULATE - One of the ingredients of the EQUATION FORMULA. This refers to the controlling of power or speed.

RELAXED MOVES - Moves that are completely relaxed in nature when utilized in an offense or defense. Tension, however, is a must at the point of contact in order to maximize back-up-mass or torque. When utilized properly, relaxed flexibility enables one to redirect movements almost effortlessly, and thus enhances spontaneity and the ability to formulate. As a further point of interest, even pain is lessened when one is in a relaxed state.

RELAYED POWER - Force that can be sustained for a longer period of time, or transferred to more than one target.

RESIDUAL MOVES - Execution of a single move that benefits you more than once.

RESIDUAL TORQUE - Multiple benefits derived from a single torquing action.

RESIDUAL WEAPON - The application of a strike that is a continuous action arising out of a check.

RESPECT - (1) Holding one in high esteem. (2) In Kenpo, saluting and bowing are symbols of respect.

RETALIATORY CHOICES - The ability to randomly select the method of execution and/or weapon prior, during (in terms of a follow-up), or after combat.

RETARDED BALL KICK - A kick that is delivered as a ball kick, but contacts with the heel of the foot (front portion) when making the initial strike.

RETARDED MOVEMENT - A movement that starts at one speed and shifts into another just prior to contact. Altered speeds during the course of a single motion, used to stifle an opponent.

RETURNING MOTION - Recoiling motion that takes alternate paths on its return, as opposed to following the same path from which it stemmed. This term is not to be confused with REVERSE MOTION.

REVERSE BOW - This stance is the reverse of the FORWARD BOW with your head and eyes turned toward your opponent. The benefits resulting from its execution are as follows: it creates instant distance, although you literally remain in place; it generates power when applying the principle of opposing forces; and it can be very useful as a leg check, buckle or break.

REVERSE MARRIAGE OF GRAVITY - Involves reversing the effects of gravity to enhance the potency of your action. Also referred to as REVERSE GRAVITATIONAL MARRIAGE.

REVERSE MOTION - returning on the same path of an initiated move.

RHYTHM - A regular recurrence of movements that follow a natural flow.

RHYTHMIC PATTERN(S) - Special designed time sequences that may be used to baffle your opponent. These patterns can be altered to add to the confusion.

RICOCHET(ING) - A glancing rebound from surface to surface or from one object to another.

RICOCHETING BLOCK - A defensive move that uses the first block to launch into a second block. This term is often interchangeably used with RICOCHETING BLOCKING STRIKE where a block is built into an aggressive strike.

RICOCHETING BLOCKING STRIKE - A single move that is first used as a block, and then launches into a strike.

RICOCHETING STRIKE - An offensive move that uses the first target to launch its action into a second target.

RIDING - A body maneuver requiring your upper body to go with an attack. This could be done while standing in place, or while retreating with the foot.

RIGHT SIDE COVER - This half cover takes place by shifting the left foot to the left (clockwise) as you turn clockwise and face the right flank. Facing 12 o'clock, whether in a right or left neutral bow, it is only the left foot that steps to the left.

RIGHT TO LEFT - A freestyle position where your right foot, which is forward, is opposite your opponent's left forward foot.

RIGHT TO RIGHT - A fighting position where both combatants face each other with their right foot forward.

RIP - Slashing motion which excludes the use of a tear.

ROLLING - Movement of one of two types: (1) (Vertical) It can be a method used when standing, where, to avoid an attack, a ride and turn are necessary to complete a maneuver. (2) (Horizontal) It can also be a revolving maneuver utilized at ground level to travel from one point to another, or to recover from a push or fall. Here, the continuous revolving flow of action helps to cushion the impact of the body when meeting the ground. This revolving maneuver may also be used to avoid an attack, by creating distance, or to strategically move into an attack, and close the distance. In either case, ROLLS revolve from a 180 degree radius to a 360 degree radius. ROLLS have the same flexibility as other methods, and can be employed simultaneously with counterattacks. As already pointed out, you can roll away from, or into a situation where the roll uses a vertical torquing action to increase body momentum. Remember, ROLLING can be done in place, or when coordinated with FOOT MANEUVERS using the ground to move you from one point to another.

ROLLING CHECK - The use of your limbs and torso to check the action and reaction of your opponent by literally rolling from one point of his body to another. Here, contact is constantly maintained in order to keep retaliation at a minimum.

ROTATE - To revolve or turn about a common axis.

ROTATING FORCE - Moves that use revolving action to contribute to their power. TORQUE is a product of ROTATING FORCE.

ROTATIONAL COCK - The rotating of the torso or limb to a more advantageous position, and in preparation for a strike that can then be executed with greater torque. See PREPARATORY TORQUE.

ROTATIONAL VELOCITY - The concept that rotation can proportionately increase the velocity of a strike.

ROUNDHOUSE - Any weapon that makes contact with its target before reaching the apex of the circular path in which it is traveling.

ROUNDING THE CORNERS - An expression used when teaching to emphasize the importance of continuing a move, so that a person does not have to stop one action in order to start another. He learns to convert the corners and points of a triangle into mini circles. It is another method used to conserve time, and aid in establishing ECONOMY OF MOTION. ▼

ROVING CHECK - Very similar to a sliding check except that the execution of this particular check does not require constant contact with your opponent's body; it can jump from one locality to another.

RULES - Generally refer to moves that must be followed to the letter. Strict adherence to the performing of such moves restricts flexibility of thought and action. Therefore, Kenpo emphasizes IDEAS or generalizations of movement rather than RULES.

RUNNING THE LINE - A method of learning self-defense techniques by forming a line and having each practitioner take his turn in doing a technique. For example, if he heads the line and is up first, he works the technique, completes it, and then goes to the end of the line to await his turn as the attacker before again becoming the defender.

RUNNING THE TABLE - A term used in the game of billiards where the player, through the use of proper positioning and alignment, hits one ball after another into the side pockets until the table is completely cleared. This analogy is used in Kenpo to emphasize the importance of proper body positioning to maximize your defensive or offensive tactics.

S

SALESMAN OF MOTION - A practitioner who can talk about the art in general, and/or in detail, but has not internalized the art to a degree at which he can use it extemporaneously.

SALUTATION - A series of moves and/or gestures in Kenpo to indicate respect for one you are greeting or competing against at a tournament.

SALUTE - (1) A term used in the titles of some techniques that employ heel palm strikes in a specific way. (2) A term describing a push from an opponent. (3) A Kenpo gesture that symbolizes respect. This is done by covering your right clenched fist with your left open hand, and then pushing both hands toward the person you wish to pay your respect to. It's a partial gesture taken out of a SALUTATION.

SANDWICHING - This involves striking  a target from opposite sides. Although both strikes are simultaneously executed, one weapon strikes and supports the action of the other. This vice like execution prevents the target from moving, and thus increases the effects of the injury. PREVENTIVE MOTION automatically occurs when employing the principle of SANDWICHING.

SCENIC ROUTE - A term used to describe taking the long way, as opposed to the short way, when executing crucial movements of combat.

SCISSORING - The use of both legs with  vice-like moves to squeeze an opponent's body as a means of confining, locking, and restricting his mobility, as well as causing discomfort and breathlessness.

SCOOP - The execution of a weapon that resembles the dipping motion of a shovel. It is literally a HOOK that is delivered vertically, and in reverse.

SCRAPING - Action which abrades and scuffs the skin of an opponent.

SCRIBBLING - Sloppy movements that are not crisp when executed. It lacks DICTION OF MOTION, and parallels movements that are MUMBLED. These moves generally occur when you are physically thinking them out in the air; instead of rattling off words, you rattle off movements.

SECOND POINT OF VIEW - This refers to your opponent's point of view. It is what he sees, and how he plans to react to what you are doing to him. If his point of view is considered in terms of what he can do to counter you and the openings that can result from such action, your chances of survival will increase proportionately.

SEE-SAW MOVES - Moves used by defender and attacker that cause them to travel back and forth.

SELF-CORRECTING - The ability to consistently make sound and logical judgments, and to act on them when analyzing movements, or when in combat situations. This can only be accomplished with a thorough knowledge of the principles, concepts and theories of the Martial Arts. Having this ability allows one to maximize his or her efforts, whether practicing, in combat, or entering some new avenue of educational expansion.

SELF-DEFENSE - The ability to protect one's self, relative, friend, or property.

SELF-DEFENSE TECHNIQUES - A series of defensive moves that are sequentially arranged to counter various types of attacks that one may encounter.

SENSEI - Japanese term for teacher, instructor, or head instructor.

SENTENCE(S) OF MOTION - Same as PARAGRAPHS OF MOTION only the techniques are shorter in length. A sequence of movements using combinations of arms and legs that are applied on one opponent.

SEQUENTIAL FLOW - This involves utilizing every conceivable natural weapon logically available within the movements of a technique sequence. Taking advantage of every natural weapon during the progress of your technique sequence not only allows your moves to flow with continuity, it teaches you how to properly COMPOUND A TECHNIQUE.

SET - (1) A term used by Chinese residing in western culture to describe a FORM. (2) SETS, like FORMS, are offensive and defensive movements incorporated into dance-like routines. Although similar in context, SETS and FORMS provide somewhat different approaches in learning the basics of Kenpo. SETS teach you how to articulate your basics, to be crisp and exact, while progressively developing them. (3) In our system of Kenpo they are appendices to the study of motion.

SET-UP - Refers to conditioning your opponent to react in a specific manner. Once this is accomplished, and his response corresponds to your desired strategic plan, it is much easier to strike and counter with effectiveness.

SETTLING - The gradual sinking of your body weight and height each time you alter the width or depth of your stance. It is a method of solidifying your base. When you solidify your base you stabilize it. This subtle maneuver adjusts the height, width, and depth of your stance, and helps increase your balance and strength. GRAVITATIONAL MARRIAGE occurs with each height adjustment.

SETTLING INTO BALANCE - The concept that your body settles each time you increase the width and depth of your stance. Balance is compensated with each change; therefore, it remains constant throughout the duration of your sequential flow of action.

SHAOLIN MONASTERY - The most famous historical temple in China. Here, many of the monks trained in the Martial Arts in the hope of recapturing China from the Manchurians and restoring it to its rightful heirs. They later became noted masters of the Arts.

SHAPE - Contour of the body.

SHOOTING THE GAP - Refers to a training method in which students line up facing each other, and advance toward, yet off-center of each other to avoid a collision. See example.

SHORINJI TEMPLE - A Japanese term for the SHAOLIN MONASTERY.

SHORT FORM I - A Form required for Yellow Belt. See FORM I.

SHORT FORM II - A Form required for Purple Belt. See FORM II.

SHORT FORM III - A Form required for Green Belt. See FORM III.

SHORTHAND MOTION - Refers to a single motion that residually accomplishes more than one purpose. A block that residually strikes, or a strike that residually blocks, all accomplished in the same motion.

SHORT RANGE WEAPONS - Natural weapons that can only be used effectively within a short distance of your opponent. Good examples of SHORT RANGE WEAPONS are the elbows and knees.

SHORT OUT - A slang expression describing black out periods during a technique sequence. These are periods of forgetfulness that cause you to stall in the course of executing a technique sequence.

SHORTENING THE CIRCLE - A method of moving up the circle to gain more reach. See MOVING UP THE CIRCLE.

SHOTOKAN - A Japanese system of Karate developed by Gichin Funakoshi.

SHOVEL KICK - A specific method of kicking, where the path of the action resembles the dipping motion of a shovel in use. This special kick allows your foot to strike two targets on the same move.

SHOVING - A push executed with explosive force.

SHUFFLE - A foot maneuver used to close or increase the distance between you and your opponent. In Kenpo there are four methods that accomplish this: push drag, drag step, step drag, and pull drag. All four methods are categorized as foot maneuvers.

SIDE COVER - Refers to a half cover that can occur either to the right or left flank. See COVER, RIGHT SIDE COVER, and LEFT SIDE COVER.

SIFU - The Chinese term for the word teacher, instructor or head instructor.

SIGNIFY - A physical gesture to indicate the number of the FORM that is about to be demonstrated. The fingers are used to indicate the specific number of the FORM that is to be displayed. Refer to FORM INDICATORS.

SIL LUM MONASTERY - A Cantonese term for the Shaolin Monastery.

SILHOUETTING - A form of CONTOURING that does not employ body contact. The formation of your torso or limbs to match the angles and curves formed by your opponent. See ANGLE MATCHING, and FRAMING.

SIMULTANEOUS - Occurring, doing, or existing at the same time. Kenpo thrives on utilizing simultaneous movements.

SINGER - One who shouts constantly. (Tournament slang.)

SINGLE LINE - A term used to have a class form a single file or column in which self-defense techniques can be practiced. The student may be asked to take on the entire line, one at a time, or alternate working on a single partner before rotating to the back of the line.

SKELETAL BONES - Human bones that form the framework that support tissues and protect the internal organs of our bodies. Knowledge of its structure, location, and strengths teaches Kenpo stylists the structural weak points of the human anatomy and determines the strategy to be used against it.

SKIP - A maneuvering method which involves moving forward, back, or sideways by skimming the ground very lightly. It is a method related to JUMPING.

SLAP - A light hit that may be used as a tool to assist your timing, as an interim move of defense, or as a minor move to set your opponent up for a major strike.

SLAPPER - One who continuously slaps his gi as a means of distraction during a match. (Tournament slang.)

SLEEPER - (1) Tournament slang for one who is a late starter. (2) A name for a Purple Belt self-defense technique. (3) Reference to the effects of a choke hold.

SLICE(ING) - An offensive maneuver in which the weapon being used skims the surface of the target being struck. This action is normally restricted to the use of a specific area of your natural weapon, where no real depth occurs during contact. However, although the depth is not as penetrating as a RAKE, it is nevertheless effective. It is basically a MINOR MOVE that is used to set your opponent up for a MAJOR MOVE.

SLIDING CHECK - A specialized PINNING BLOCK that travels on an opponent's body by sliding from one leverage point to another. During the course of each slide, constant body contact is maintained (body contouring) to avoid retaliation. This is technically a form of CONTOURING.

SLIP(PING) - (1) To slide off balance. (2) The insertion of an aggressive move to a target without your opponent being aware of its execution. (3) A method of avoiding an attack while going toward your opponent's action. This may be done directly or indirectly. That is you can SLIP past and toward your opponent at the very start of an attack, or RIDE the attack first, before SLIPPING toward the action.

SLOW MOVES - Moves that are taught slowly to beginners who need to learn precision and proper synchronization of the body. Learning moves slowly helps to eliminate bad habits.

SMOTHER PUNCH - A specific method of executing a punch so that it appears to smother its target.

SNAKING MOVES - Defensive moves that twist and turn as they wind around or intertwine with the attacking weapons of your opponent.

SNAP(PING) - A method of execution requiring the natural weapon to dart out and back with crispness and energy. It involves greater magnitude than the action of a WHIP. See WHIP.

SOFT - Refers to moves that are applied with little force. They are flexible moves that generally sting, but do not injure. These are MINOR MOVES that are useful set ups for moves that strike with greater magnitude.

SOFT STYLE - A system that primarily employs moves de-emphasizing power, while utilizing speed to great advantage.

SOLIDIFY YOUR BASE - Means to strengthen your stance so that it is both firm and strong.

SOPHISTICATED BASICS - A single basic move that produces multiple results.

SOPHISTICATED SIMPLICITY - The ability to compound simple basics into multiple action. Moves that appear to have only one purpose, but actually produce a number of results.

SOUTHERN SYSTEMS (STYLES) - Generally refers to those Martial Arts systems practiced in Southern China. These systems concentrated more on hand movements than on foot movements.

SPECIALIZED METHODS - A further subdivision of SPECIALIZED MOVES. These catagories describe the manners in which SPECIALIZED MOVES may be applied. For instance, one might administer a pinching or a sandwiching VICE-LIKE move; a jerking or a tearing PULL; a pressing or nudging PUSH; or a sweeping or buckling UN-BALANCING move.

SPECIALIZED MOVES - Although there are specialized applications within each of the four major categories of BASICS (STANCES, MANEUVERS, BLOCKS, and STRIKES), they are no more than combinations stemming from each of these categories. The major category of SPECIALIZED MOVES stands alone, and embodies four major subdivisions: VICE-LIKE moves, PUSHING moves, PULLING moves, UN-BALANCING moves. Each of these subdivisions, in turn, have more specific applications. (See SPECIALIZED METHODS.)

SPEED - Generally refers to increased acceleration of the body when engaged in action. The faster the acceleration, the greater the force. However, there are three categories of speed — perceptual, mental, and physical (body performance). Although categorized separately, for purposes of analyzing what speed entails, they nevertheless function as one. See PERCEPTUAL, MENTAL, and PHYSICAL SPEED, as well as QUICKNESS.

SPIN - A specialized foot maneuver requiring the body to make a full 360 degree turn while executing an attack, avoiding an attack, or escaping from an opponent.

SPINNER - One who uses an excessive amount of spinning back kicks or spinning back knuckles. (Tournament slang.)

SPIRALING - Action requiring the body to descend with each turn or spin.

SPIRALING STAIRCASE - A concept of movement in which the action follows the path of a spiraling staircase. When applied properly, the height zone of your opponent is constantly kept in check, and the execution of the move flows with ease and continuity.

SPIRIT - (1) Disposition of the mind. (2) To move with vitality.

SPIRIT OF THE ATTACK - That stage, when practicing a technique, that requires realistic application on the part of your attacking partner. It becomes increasingly beneficial to first, second, and third person point of view when your partner's actions are delivered with vigor, zest, and SPIRIT.

SPIRIT OF THE TECHNIQUE - That stage, when practicing a technique, that requires realistic, vigorous, and spirited application of moves in your role as the defender. At this point, it is to your advantage to approach application of the technique (within reason) as though you were in a life and death situation.

SPIRITUAL SENSITIVITY - A level of mental development wherein the harmonious unification of the conscious and subconscious minds allows one unrestricted perceptual latitude.

SPIT SHINE - Slang term referring to the polishing of a technique, improving one's basics, or sophisticating one's techniques or skills.

SPONTANEOUS - Refers to moves of impulse. Instinctive reactions triggered by the subconscious mind.

SPONTANEOUS STAGE - The stage where the student's reactions are executed naturally, impulsively and without restraint, effort, or premeditation.

SPRINGBOARD - A move or action that uses your or your opponent's body, or the ground, floor, wall, etc. to help launch your next move or action.

SQUEEGEE PRINCIPLE - Principle that stresses using the PATH of your action to cover a wider area when blocking or striking. Such action allows you greater margin for error. Refer to UPPER and LOWER CASE OF MOTION.

SQUEEZE - A method that requires grabbing and compressing specific areas on an opponent's body.

STABILIZE YOUR BASE - Similar to SOLIDIFY YOUR BASE with stress placed on balance.

STAFF - A long pole made of wood that is used as a weapon.

STAFF FORM - Requirement for 2nd Degree Brown Belt.

STAGES OF DISTANCE - Varying distances that occur during combat that can be increased or decreased via the use of foot maneuvers.

STANCE(S) - Postural positions of the legs and body that can be formed or structured prior, during, or after combat.

STANCE SET I - A set required for Purple Belt.

STANCE SET II - A set required for Third Degree Brown Belt.

STAR BLOCK - Another name for BLOCKING SET I, and a requirement for Yellow Belt. It is a blocking exercise that is done from a horse stance.

STATIONARY - To remain in place.

STATES OF MOTION - (SOLID-LIQUID-GAS)

STEP - The moving of the front foot forward, or the rear foot back, to increase the depth or width of a stance. It may also involve moving the right foot to the right, or the left foot to the left, depending on one's purpose(s).

STEP BACK - Another term used to describe a STEP THROUGH foot maneuver when taking one full step back.

STEP-DRAG - The stepping forward, or back, with one foot and the dragging of the other foot so that the distance between them returns to their original depth. This is another of the methods of shuffling.

STEP-THROUGH - The execution of full steps, by either moving forward or back. In the case of a step through kick, it means kicking with the forward foot and planting it to your rear, or kicking with the rear foot and planting it to your front.

STICK(S) - Generally refers to batons made of rattan that are used by practitioners of Escrima or Arnis.

STIFF LOCK-OUT - Strategic action used to cause your limbs (arm or leg) to become firm and rigid at the precise moment they are stretched to their limit. This is done to either impose a time deterrent (momentary delay against retaliation), or to enhance, as well as conclude, the effects of a lifting strike.

STOMPING - A thrusting method using the foot to strike down toward targets located on or near the ground.

STORM - A term used in self-defense techniques to refer to a club attack.

STRATEGIC PLOY - Calculated bid or action designed to draw an assailant into following a plan to your benefit, and/or to his disadvantage.

STREETFIGHTER - Generally refers to an individual who has no formal training, and who enjoys fighting on the street. He does not believe in ethics, and his philosophy on the street is that "anything goes" even if weapons were needed to insure his victory.

STREET FREESTYLE(IST) - Kenpo stylists who are formally trained in the ways of streetfighting. Moves are learned scientifically to insure the best results, in the shortest time, against one or more aggressors. Rules do not exist in such encounters.

STRETCHING - Exercise methods used to extend and stretch the muscles before engaging in heavy workout. ▼

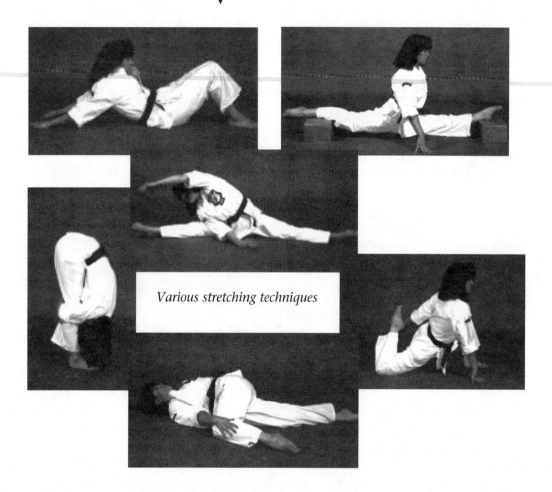

Various stretching techniques

STRETCH REFLEX - Warning given to tendon receptors to prevent over-stretching of a muscle.

STRIKE(S) - Methods used to execute NATURAL WEAPONS. VITAL TARGETS can be punched, kicked, chopped, poked, hammered, etc.

STRIKEDOWNS - Many styles of the Martial Arts use takedowns to force their opponent to the ground. Takedowns utilize throwing actions to force an opponent to the ground, and it is the impact with the ground that causes the initial injury. Although considered a takedown, strikedowns are much more effective. Since you are striking your opponent to the ground, his injury occurs instantly, as well as with the resultant impact with the ground. Strikedowns are often counterbalanced with buckles.

STRIKING BLOCK - Any block that bucks or goes against the force of an opponent's strike.

STRIKING SET I - A set required for Blue Belt.

STRIKING SET II - A set required for 1st Degree Brown Belt.

STRUCTURAL REINFORCEMENT - Same as BRACING ANGLE. Also refer to IMPACT, ADJUSTMENT, BALANCE COMPENSATION, and BACK-UP-MASS.

STUTTERING MOTION - Motion that is deliberately used to disrupt the thought patterns of an opponent during combat. They are premeditated movements of disrupted rhythm, otherwise known as BROKEN RHYTHM, which combines both FEINTING and deliberate movements to defeat an opponent.

STYLE - Is the word used to describe the manner in which an individual applies and executes the system he has learned. Although the underlying principles are the same, they are nevertheless altered to suit the individual.

SUBCONSCIOUS - That reservoir of knowledge that remains just beyond the reach of normal consciousness. It is when the conscious and subconscious merge that the genie within you comes to the surface; therein, lies your answer to attaining Ki or Chi.

SUFFIX(ING) - The addition of a move or moves immediately after the BASE MOVE. You have probably been introduced to this idea through the development of freestyle techniques. Naturally, you may have picked up a few ideas about suffixing self-defense techniques by watching and practicing with more advanced students. Learning to suffix can add new fun and excitement to your art; it can look good, and it can impress others. However, at this point we must caution you. Please remember, you must have a solid base move. If a technique sequence does not seem to be working for you, do not compound your problem by adding to it. Develop good basics, understand the idea of each technique, train properly, and develop a positive attitude. Then you will gain the benefits of suffixing some of which are:
1. Suffixes help to keep your opponent mentally and physically off balance.
2. Suffixes reduce your opponent's ability to retaliate.
3. They adhere to the principles of Continuous Weapons and Continuity of Motion.

4. They provide additional Diversified Weapons to insure multiple effects.
5. They teach you to continue your action if your original ideas are ineffective or checked by your opponent.
6. They increase your Vocabulary of Motion by utilizing new weapons, new targets, new angles of execution, new methods of execution, etc. . . .
7. They increase your flexibility of thought.
8. They may be very useful transitions during encounters with multiple attackers.
9. Suffixes teach you how to work with an opponent who is on the way to the ground.
10. They teach you how to work an opponent who is on the ground.
11. They teach you how to provide the final touches to your "full course meal".
12. Suffixes build the responses necessary to continue the action no matter which positions you or your opponent may be in during combat.

SUGGESTED APPROACHES - Refers to the study of motion through logic, continuity, and economy of motion, all of which provide flexibility in making on-the-spot decisions.

SUPERCONSCIOUS STATE - The highest level of the SPONTANEOUS STAGE. This state is created when the conscious and subconscious minds harmonize and work as one to bring about that genie which is in each of us. When brought to the surface, this genie performs beyond the limits placed upon our natural or normal self.

SUPERLEARNING - A reference text that is quoted in Volume IV of Infinite Insights into Kenpo.

SURFACE CONCENTRATION - This term refers to the impact force between weapon and target and the resulting stresses that occur. It follows the principle of a pin or a nail where the surface of the natural weapon being used is as small an area as possible in order to have a more penetrating effect on the target. While the surface injury is at a minimum, the internal effects are much greater.

SURVEY - To observe, to have an overview of an attack before making a retaliatory commitment.

SWEEPER - One who likes to sweep his opponent as part of his technique. (Tournament slang.)

SWEEPING CHECK - Any method used with either arm or leg that sweeps the path of action to insure a check.

SWITCH - In place exchange of lead legs while facing the same direction. This is done by exchanging foot positions from one spot to another. Three alternatives can be used in making the exchange, (1) you can step back to front (2) step front to back, or (3) jump in place.

SWORDHAND - Is a natural weapon using the knife-edge of the hand. See HANDSWORD which is the more acceptable term.

SYMMETRICAL - Where one half is equal to the other in looks, balance, shape, etc. In the case of a horse stance, one side is identical to the other. This term is related to CORRESPONDING ANGLES, where the shape or position of one body limb matches the angle that's shaped or positioned by another. For example the position of your arm may match or parallel the angle of your leg. CORRESPONDING ANGLES also fall under the heading of CONTOURING, and enhance the balance of your transitional moves. Also refer to ANGLE MATCHING and SILHOUETTING.

SYNC - Precise merger of thought, mind, and breath; or principles, action, and forces. Refer to IN SYNC.

SYNCHRONIZED - To move or occur at the same time or rate; to cause to agree in time or rate of speed.

SYNCHRONIZATION - (1) Refers to an opponent coordinating his moves, timing, and direction with yours in order to take advantage of them, and to attack you. (2) The tying together of moves so that they become one.

SYSTEM - The unification of related concepts, truths, and basic elements of a particular school of Martial Arts. SYSTEM is the method whereas STYLE is the application or execution of the method.

T

TACKLING - A vice-like method used to seize and throw an opponent to the ground.

TAE KWON DO - A Korean system of Karate that concentrates primarily on kicks and hand movements that are predominantly linear.

TAILORED - Altered, adapted, or fitted to the environment, circumstance, or capability of the individual concerned.

TAILORING - This is one of the key principles of Kenpo. It entails two major aspects, (1) adjusting your physical as well as mental and emotional attitudes to fit each given situation; and (2) fitting moves to your body size, makeup, speed, and strength in order to maximize your physical efforts.

TAKEDOWN MANEUVERS - Defensive or offensive moves used to strike or force an opponent to the ground. Taking such action can immobilize, restrain, control, or prevent further attack.

TALON - A term used in self-defense techniques referring to a wrist grab.

TAN'G HANDS - A term used to describe some of the Korean Martial Art Systems during a specific period of their history. T'ang Hand, named out of respect to China, literally means the hand of China.

TAN'G SOO DO - Another Korean system of Karate named out of respect to China.

TANGENT - The meeting of a straight line with a curved surface. In Kenpo language, it is the meeting of a linear strike with a curved target, which diverges from the original purpose, or course, of the intended action.

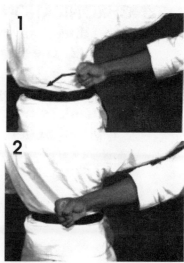

TARGET AREAS - See TARGETS.

TARGET PLACEMENT - (1) The ability to place a target in an ideal position or posture whereby your natural weapon(s) can render a more effective strike. (2) You may also use strategic movements to place yourself in an opportune position that will allow you a clear path to the target of your choice.

TARGETS - Important areas on your or your opponent's body which when struck can be injured or damaged. See *Infinite Insights into Kenpo, Volume 4, Mental & Physical Constituents* Pages 66-71 for further detailed description.

TARGETS TO OBJECTS - The use of environmental objects as weapons to injure an opponent. To accomplish this, effective techniques are employed to guide and force assailants into environmental objects that can injure.

TE - An Okinawan term which means hand. Their Art was originally called Okinawa-te or Hand Art of Okinawa.

TEA KETTLE PRINCIPLE - This teaches that the expulsion of air when striking should be controlled so that it is condensed or shortened. If we compare our bodies and normal breathing with a tea kettle and the steam that is released through its spout, we will see that greater condensation yields greater energy. (See ANALOGY OF TEA KETTLE). With the tea kettle, the condensation is produced by the fixed chamber of the kettle (only so much air can escape through the spout) and the amount of heat beneath it. If the variable of heat is increased enough, eventually the lid would be propelled from the kettle by the steam's expansion. In the case of our bodies the condensation is produced through the contraction of our abdominal and throat muscles (we change the size of the kettle and its spout instead of its contents). As a result of the increased energy in our bodies (like the steam in the kettle), we propel our strikes with a greater force. In short, condensed breathing, like condensed steam under pressure, proportionately increases the force rendered.

TEAR - Ripping motion which actually involves grabbing while pulling.

TECHNICIAN OF MOTION - A practitioner who has the ability to dissect, analyze, scrutinize, and internalize motion to a point where he can also teach others to do the same.

TECHNIQUE - Pre-planned moves that can be used defensively or offensively with successful results. See SELF-DEFENSE TECHNIQUE(S).

TECHNIQUE LINE - Same as RUNNING THE LINE.

TECHNIQUE SEQUENCE - A planned combination of moves which may be used defensively or offensively.

TECHNIQUES IN THE AIR - Refers to practicing self-defense techniques without a partner. Training in this manner requires visualizing an imaginary opponent attacking you, and then applying defensive and offensive moves in answer to his attack. Executing techniques properly in empty space (in the air) requires imagination and a great deal of practice. You must be focused on the point where each move of your composed sequence is to be placed, in addition to anticipating your opponent's reaction stemming from these moves. This in no way refers to AIR-BORNE TECHNIQUES.

TELEGRAPHING - This is a body language that often works against you. These movements can warn your opponent of your intended action, and help him prepare his defense. TELEGRAPHING, however, can work for you when used strategically to deceive your opponent, and causing him to misread your true intentions.

TELEPATHICALLY - Describes a method of understanding or conveying knowledge or intentions through no outward or physical signs.

TENDONS - Bands of tough, fibrous connective tissue forming the termination of a muscle, and serving to transmit its force to some other part.

THEORY - An idea needing further research and analysis to prove its validity. A hypothetical idea needing experimentation to make it a factual PRINCIPLE.

THEORY OF PROPORTIONAL DIMENSION - This theory teaches you how to utilize movements which are in proportion to your body. Applying this theory helps you to, literally, fit the moves to your body. When used as a training tool, it can aid you in finding the proper dimensions of height, width, and depth as it applies to your stances, blocks, etc. As you learn to proportionately fit your stances to your body, stability and maneuverability become unrestrained. Applying this theory to your defensive and offensive movements can cause your moves to instinctively follow paths that are proportionate to the structure and contour of your and/or your opponent's body. (See TAILORING.)

THESIS - (1) A written research paper. (2) As part of their examination for promotion in the International Kenpo Karate Association, students are required, at different levels of their progress, to compose and write a thesis and/or create a FORM of their own. Mr. Parker's concept of writing a thesis and creating a FORM is designed to help students develop individual creativity. In fulfilling this requirement, they are compelled to think; therefore, students are required to analyze each and every effort they make. In completing this assignment, it is hoped that students will be motivated to become critical of themselves, and strive for self-perfection. Through self-analyzation and their quest for perfection, they learn to be individualists who can function independently. In a real crisis, their independence will allow them to remain cool, steadfast, and quick while making decisions which will ultimately lead to victory.

WRITTEN THESIS

Students may choose the subject matter for their written thesis. It can be on any subject related to the Martial Arts. On rare occasions, Mr. Parker will select a subject related to their skill, profession or hobby if he feels it will benefit all members of the Association. If a specific subject is selected, students will be notified in ample time so that they can complete their thesis prior to the deadline.

If students cannot decide upon a topic, or in the event that they have an array of topics which they would like to choose from, but are having difficulty making a decision, they are to consult with their Instructor for his recommendation. His suggestions are important in any case.

Each student's educational background will be considered in evaluating their written thesis. Therefore, more will be expected of them if they have higher academic credentials. All students, however, will be required to follow the format outlined in the following paragraphs.

The following information serves as a guide in the presentation of their required written thesis. It is their responsibility to organize and develop their thesis in the foregoing manner. Suggestions are not given in terms of their writing, but only on how to present their facts.

FORMAT — Their thesis shall consist of three main parts. The following must be adhered to:

1. PRELIMINARY PAGES

    (a) TITLE PAGE (followed by a blank page). This page should include:
        (1) The name of the studio along with its branch name directly under it. (Both should be centered at the top of the page.)
        (2) The exact title of the thesis;
        (3) The belt promotion it is for;
        (4) The date;
        (5) Their name as the author — all suitably capitalized, centered, and spaced upon the page. (See illustrated sample.)

(b) PREFACE AND/OR ACKNOWLEDGEMENTS — Included in the preface (or forward) should be their reasons for picking their topic; for making the study; the background, scope, and references; an acknowledgement to those who have aided them in the process of their research. If they think they have nothing significant to say about their thesis, and wish to acknowledge the assistance they have received, they should entitle their remarks "Acknowledgements" instead of "Preface". (See illustrated sample.)

(c) TABLE OF CONTENTS — This is basically an outline setting forth the major divisions of the thesis: the introduction, the chapters, the glossary, the appendix, and the bibliography, with their respective page numbers. (See illustrated sample.)

(d) LIST OF ILLUSTRATIONS — The list of illustrations should be placed on a separate page. There should be a number, title, and page number for each illustration.

2. THE TEXT shall consist of an:

(a) INTRODUCTION — It should lead into the main body of the paper.

(b) THE MAIN BODY of the paper. This is the actual meat of the thesis. Should the thesis be lengthy, divisions, such as chapters or their equivalent should be used to divide the text. Each chapter should have a title and begin on a new page.

3. REFERENCE MATERIAL SHOULD CONSIST OF:

(a) A BIBLIOGRAPHY — The bibliography is a listing of all of the sources used in the writing of the thesis. Just those relevant to the subject should be listed.

(b) A GLOSSARY — The glossary should list all specialized terminology utilized in the thesis, in alphabetical order, with their accompanying definitions.

(c) AN APPENDIX — The appendix should contain all supplementary information pertinent to the formation of the thesis, but would be inappropriate elsewhere. This might include how a model was constructed, or the method or means of acquiring certain information, etc.

THESIS ABSTRACT

Each student testing for Third Degree Brown Belt shall be required to present an abstract of the thesis they intend to write for First Degree Black Belt. This abstract is a brief one or two page statement about their proposed thesis and should include:

1. Verification of the approval of their topic by their instructor. It is important that their subject matter be a worthy one, one that is sufficient in depth, and that they are capable of completing.

2. A tentative title for their thesis.

3. One or two paragraphs highlighting the proposed subject, and an explanation of how they intend to cover their subject in greater depth.

4. A paragraph explaining why they have chosen this topic.

5. A list of their intended sources of information.

Their Thesis Abstract must be presented to their instructor at least two weeks prior to testing. This will allow time for him to approve its form and content, and allow the student time to make revisions. The final Abstract must be presented by their instructor to Mr. Parker prior to their test with sufficient time for Mr. Parker to read and approve it.

THE FINAL THESIS

The primary goal of all members of the International Kenpo Karate Association should be to learn Mr. Parker's system. A vital part of Kenpo's educational process involves sharing one's own knowledge, perspectives, and insights; thus, each individual contributes to the overall development of our system. One means of achieving this goal is through the student's black belt thesis.

The final thesis for First Degree Black Belt candidates should be concise, accurate, and to the point. Although there is no minimum length required, their topic should be of sufficient depth to require several type-written pages. Each written thesis MUST BE COMPLETED and presented to the candidate's instructor at least two weeks prior to testing. This will allow time for the instructor to approve its form and content, and allow the student time to make revisions. The final thesis must then be presented by the instructor to Mr. Parker prior to the test and with sufficient time for Mr. Parker to read and approve it. This will enable Mr. Parker to question or comment on it during the exam.

THIRD POINT OF VIEW - This refers to a bystander's point of view. It is how he views the encounter. As you develop sequential patterns of defense and offense it is highly recommended that you consider his point of view, for it may reveal other existing openings or uses of natural weapons that you may have otherwise overlooked. This point of view increases your ability to observe additional openings or counters that you may have missed if you were only to consider the FIRST and SECOND POINTS OF VIEW.

THREADING - A means of CONTOURING where a joint of your body is used to guide the natural weapon of your choice to its target. This can only occur if the two body parts that form the joint meet each other at specific angles so as to warrant its use. Instead of TRACKING its way to the target, inch by inch, the natural weapon remains on one spot as it THREADS its way to the target.

THREE PHASE CONCEPT - The concept that no technique is a set pattern or rule unto itself, but rather is composed of THREE PHASES — IDEAL (PHASE I), WHAT IF (PHASE II), and FORMULATION (PHASE III). Please refer to each of these listed PHASES.

THREE POINTS OF VIEW - See VIEWPOINT. Also refer to FIRST POINT OF VIEW, SECOND POINT OF VIEW, and THIRD POINT OF VIEW.

THRUST - A particular method of execution used to propel a strike. It resembles an explosive push type action.

THROWING - (1) Methods using leverage and counter manipulation to hurl an opponent to the ground. (2) Methods used to hurl objects or man made weapons such as a knife, star, etc.

TIGER - A symbol used in Kenpo to represent earthly strength derived during the early stages of learning. This is the stage where the individual is more impressed with his own physical prowess. Refer to KENPO CREST.

TIGER CLAW - A natural weapon of the hand that uses the finger tips to claw with.

TIGER'S MOUTH - A specific way of forming the hand for squeezing that resembles the mouth of a tiger. This hand formation can be found in the technique RAINING LANCE.

TIGHT - Condition of severe restraint or abnormal tension, and where muscles are not necessarily firm. To be abnormally stiff and tense mentally, as well as physically. See CONSTIPATED MOVES.

TIGHT VS. TONED - TIGHT is the abnormal tension of the body, whereas TONED refers to the normal and natural tension of the body.

TIME COMPRESSION - The ability to reduce the time and effectiveness of your action. It is a contributing ingredient that enhances ECONOMY OF MOTION.

TIME DETERRENT - The execution of a move to keep an opponent's timing off or behind the normal synchronized time pattern, so that he has to re-set himself before he can continue his normal action. For example, a heel palm jab can set your opponent back at least one half beat, and thus delay him from FILLING THE GAP.

TIMING - Is the sophistication and punctuation of rhythm.

TIPS - Corresponding strips of colored cloth that are placed on gi belts to designate the level or degree of a particular belt rank.

TOE/HEEL LINE- Method of determining the proper width of a NEUTRAL BOW AND ARROW STANCE, where the toe of the forward foot is in line with the heel of the rear foot.

TONED - The body in its natural state of tension, where muscles are firm as well as strong.

TONGS - Are Chinese syndicates or associations organized to accomplish specific tasks that benefit their members.

TORQUE - Twisting and rotating action used to position your body and muscles to work at maximum efficiency. See ROTATING FORCE.

TOTAL PHYSICAL HARMONY - See BODY HARMONY.

TOUCH - Refers to your ability to physically feel an object. It is the sense of physically feeling. It also refers to very light contact, a rule that is often required at Karate tournaments.

TOURNAMENT FREESTYLE - Sparring that is conducted at a tournament where specific rules must be adhered to. TOURNAMENT FREESTYLE varies nationally and internationally. Some abide by no contact, light contact, or full contact rules.

TRACKING - Is a more specific way of CON-TOURING that is used to obtain precisioned accuracy. It normally follows a limb of the body that is already on target, so that the accuracy of your follow-up is guaranteed. For example, if your were executing a right two finger hook to your opponent's left eye, you could leave it on target so that your left hand could follow the contour of your right arm in order to accurately poke the same eye. Timing in this instance is crucial. Simultaneously, as your right hook leaves your opponent's eye, your left finger poke must make contact to the very same target. Switching weapons at the last minute makes the second strike obscure. Contrary to GUIDELINING it follows a line of action.

TRADITIONAL - Generally refers to Martial Art practitioners who adhere to custom, and who firmly believe in the original concepts and moves of a particular system. Unfortunately, strict reliance to these classical methods often restrict creativity, self expression, and the ability to alter with our ever changing environment.

TRAILING - A method whereby the second movement [(strike), hand, foot, or person] is delayed one or more beats behind that of the starting action. This delay could take place when moving forward, in reverse, or when employing combinations of both. The principle of TRAILING can also enhance the employment of variable expansion. TRAILING also works when traveling to the right or left when performing sets. It is an overlooked principle that can be useful in allowing larger groups to simultaneously perform in a confined area.

TRAILING LEG - The leg that always remains to the rear of the LEAD LEG. The back leg, or leg that is to the rear of the lead leg.

TRANSFER OF EYESIGHT - This is the concept that once you have visualized where your opponent's height, width, and depth zones are located, his postural changes should have no bearing on the accuracy of your natural weapon, whatever the desired target may be. The concept teaches you to transfer your eye(s) to whatever weapon you plan to employ, and to have it view the intended target to determine the approach and method it should employ.

TRANSFORMATIVE MOVE(S) - The ability to deceptively change an element of a move or sequence after conditioning your opponent to view it one way. His conditioned response will cause the change to go unnoticed. TRANSFORMATIVE MOVES are necessary in creating HEIGHT, DEPTH and WIDTH DECEPTION.

TRANSITION - The stage between moves; moves within moves.

TRANSITIONAL MOVES - The in-between moves of a technique that can also supply important answers in terms of defense or offense. These answers lie dormant within the transition of your sequential flow. They can surface anytime you desire while moving toward or away from your opponent. Transitions can work well in a SET or FORM, where the last move of the first technique could be employed as the first move of the second technique, or vice versa.

TRANSITIONAL RESPONSE - The ability to rapidly blanket your opponent's action(s), so that your response to each of his moves effectively counters them.

TRANSITORY MOVE(S) - In-between move(s) that often take place when moving from one position to another. Their employment can be crucial in certain instances, and, often produces dual effects.

TRANSITORY STANCE(S) - Temporary stance used to move from one stance to another.

TRANSITORY STRIKES - same definition as TRANSITORY MOVES.

TRAP(PING) - Is any stratagem designed to CATCH a natural weapon and prevent it from escaping.

TRIPPING - Quick methods used to cause an opponent to stumble.

TUCK - To draw the head, arms, or body into a more compact position.

TWIG - A term used in self-defense techniques to refer to the arm.

TWIN FACTOR - Identical weapons (natural) being employed simultaneously.

TWINS - A term used in self-defense techniques to indicate two identical strikes being delivered simultaneously.

TWIRLING - A specialized foot maneuver that requires spinning the body clockwise or counterclockwise while in the air in order to travel from one ground point to another. Both the upper and lower body are synchronized to TWIRL simultaneously while moving toward or away from your opponent.

TWIRLING CHECK - Use of rotating moves that continuously contour, as well as contact the body of an opponent to keep his retaliatory efforts in check.

TWIST(ING) - (1) To rotate or turn in place. (2) Application of torsional stress so as to sprain, distort, dislocate, or break a wrist, ankle, neck, etc.

TWIST STANCE - A short term used to describe the TWISTED HORSE STANCE. This stance can be formed from a HORSE STANCE by rapidly twisting the waist and allowing the feet to pivot freely.

TWO-MAN FORM - Requirement for 2nd Degree Brown Belt.

UNCOMMITTED ACTION - Moves that are not committed to taking a specific course of action. Freedom to take action at any time, to any target, in any manner desired.

UNCONCERNED POSITIONS - These are unprepared positions assumed while one is unconscious of trouble or danger.

UNIFY - The bringing together of forces, or of the mind, breath, and strength, etc.

UNINTENTIONAL MOVES - Unanticipated reactionary moves on the part of an opponent that, although accidental or unplanned, can cause injury if they remain unchecked.

UNIVERSAL BLOCK - A specific block that simultaneously employs two types of arm blocks to complete the defense.

UNIVERSAL PATTERN - A three dimensional pattern of movements conceived and developed by Ed Parker as a directional key to movement. This extensive pattern is a useful learning tool to enhance students' knowledge of motion. It is also a design that can aid you in systematically understanding the interrelationship of linear and circular movements and the paths in which they travel. Once understood it can be applied to self-defense techniques, forms, freestyle, etc. As you learn to correlate moves within the

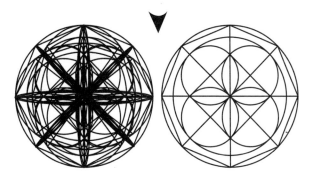

3 Dimensional Universal Pattern using 9 planes, also a more commonly known, (heart up) 2 Dimensional 1 plane, Universal Pattern.

pattern, alternative moves become instinctive and spontaneous. You must not, however, get caught up in the manner of study, but the reasons involved within the study.

UNUSEFUL - Movements that may not be useful in one predicament, but can be in another. They may be unuseful in one combat situation, but positively effective in another.

UNWIND(ING) - To uncoil or rotate in reverse. Uncoiling from a TWIST STANCE can be effective if the momentum of the rotation is synchronized with a strike.

UPPER CASE MOVEMENT - (1) This term refers to the fact that movements, like the letters of the alphabet, can have UPPER (CAPITAL LETTERS) and LOWER (small letters) CASES.(2) This concept also closely parallels the SQUEEGEE PRINCIPLE. For example, if you are blocking a high strike with the hammer portion of your fist, you are urged not to use the same part of your hand to block a second blow that may be aimed at the stomach. Instead, you are urged to use the lower part of your forearm, since it is closer to the line of action of the second blow, and affords greater ECONOMY OF MOTION. The employment of an UPPER CASE MOVEMENT followed by a LOWER CASE MOVEMENT would have your arm following a path of action as opposed to following a line of action, and would allow you greater MARGIN FOR ERROR. Also refer to MARGIN FOR ERROR, PATH, PATH OF ACTION, SQUEEGEE PRINCIPAL and LOWER CASE MOVEMENT. See lower case movement.

UPPERCUT - An upward vertical motion used to execute a punch.

UPSIDE OF MOVEMENT - Going up the circle has bearing on extending the upside of the movement. (See UPSIDE OF MOVEMENT VS. UPSIDE OF CIRCLE.)

UPSIDE OF THE CIRCLE - Refers to making contact with your target prior to reaching the apex of your circle (path in which your weapon is traveling). This is the type of action used to create a ROUNDHOUSE punch or kick. (See DOWNSIDE OF THE CIRCLE.)

UPSIDE OF MOVEMENT VS. UPSIDE OF THE CIRCLE - The upside of your movement is the furthest distance achieved when employing your lead hand as your weapon, and as your rear foot moves on the upside of your circle. See illustration.

UPWARD BLOCK(S) - All types of blocks that redirect an attacking weapon up, above, over, out, or away from your head.

USE(ING) - Another word in Kenpo to describe apply(ing) or employ(ing).

USEFUL - Any logical or practical move that can be effectively used.

USELESS - This term is not the same as UNUSEFUL. These are moves that are not effective under any condition.

"V" STEP - Use of step-through foot maneuvers that follow the directional path with the shape of a "V".

VARIABLE EXPANSION - The ability to randomly select solutions, or build upon precepts, as a result of having a thorough knowledge of the principles and concepts of the Martial Arts.

VELOCITY - Time rate, or speed of linear motion in a given direction.

VENETIAN BLIND PRINCIPLE - Teaches how zones on the body can decrease or increase in size, like a venetian blind, when the angle of the body changes in height and width.

VERSATILITY OF ACTION - The ability to randomly change from one method of execution to another without disrupting the flow of your movements. Grafted Principles and Grafted techniques are examples of Versatility of Action.

VERTICAL PLANE - Upright, straight up and down plane.

VERTICAL OUTWARD BLOCK - A type of block used for CLOSE RANGE ENCOUNTERS, and that sends the attacking weapon out and away from you.

VERTICAL ZONES - One of the three categorical ZONES OF PROTECTION. It encompasses four vertical or width segments that need to be protected; (1) left outside shoulder to middle of left chest, (2) Middle of left chest to sternum, (3) Sternum to middle of right chest, (4) Middle of right chest to outside of right shoulder. This term is synonymous with WIDTH ZONES.

VICE-LIKE MOVES - Moves that compress, squeeze, pinch, or have a sandwiching effect.

VIEWPOINT - This entails viewing a confrontation from three points of view: yours, that of your opponent, and the bystander who may be witnessing the event. Utilizing this concept will illuminate many avenues of offense and defense that would have otherwise been missed.

VISUAL INTERPRETATION - What you conceive to be, in light of what you are witnessing. Your belief or assessment of what you have witnessed.

VITAL AREAS - The major weak points of the body.

VITAL TARGETS - Points on your or your opponent's anatomy that can be greatly affected, injured, maimed, or cause death when struck. See TARGET AREAS.

VOCABULARY OF MOTION - Refers to having an extensive knowledge of Martial Art movements. Each individual move, whether they be offensive or defensive, is considered to be a letter in the ALPHABET OF MOTION. Combinations using the same arm or foot form WORDS OF MOTION. Combinations employing both hands and/or both feet are considered SENTENCES OF MOTION. Combined SENTENCES OF MOTION form PARAGRAPHS OF MOTION. These combinations create an almost infinite number of alternatives, and the more versed a martial artist is in those alternatives, the more fluent his response to any physical confrontation.

W

WALL PAINTER - Tournament slang for those who compete while continuously using vertical movements with their hands.

WASTED MOTION - Motion which has no appreciable effect.

WEAPON ALIGNMENT - The specific positioning of a natural weapon prior to delivery. See POSITIONAL ALIGNMENT, POSITIONAL AIM and POSITIONAL COCK.

WEAPON AVAILABILITY - The proper positioning of natural weapons for immediate use.

WEAVE(ING) - A body maneuver used to avoid an attack while horizontally moving the upper body from side to side toward a number of angles or directions.

WEB OF KNOWLEDGE - The pattern of a web 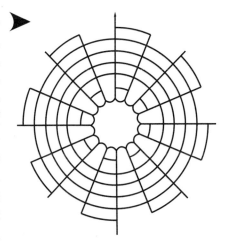 created, developed, designed, and used by Ed Parker to prioritize self-defense techniques according to the degree of difficulty in handling an attack. This postulate teaches you to (1) identify, define, and classify the types of encounters you may find yourself in; (2) thoroughly scrutinize the various methods in which weapons (natural or otherwise) can be employed; and (3) instinctively determine your choice of action to successfully combat the numerous types of encounters with which you may be confronted.

When identifying the nature of an attack, you must: (1) ascertain whether trouble is eminent in the ENVIRONMENT you are entering; (2) anticipate the possibility of an encounter; and (3) eliminate the element of surprise. Although the type of action you encounter may surprise you, you should, nevertheless, be prepared to instinctively utilize your knowledge regardless of the predicament.

At an advanced stage, strategy and plans for defense and offense are not thought of consciously — they occur naturally. For the beginner, however, defining the predicament involves consciously classifying and categorizing the various types of attack, so that he can better utilize his more limited and less familiar set of tools. Answers are more appropriately geared to attack situations when they are categorized into topics such as:

1. Grabs and Tackles
2. Pushes
3. Punches
4. Kicks
5. Holds and Hugs
6. Locks and Chokes
7. Weapons
8. Multiple Attacks

While these categories become extremely helpful in defining the attack, they, nevertheless, are general categories. Specific detailing is needed since there are numerous methods of executing the techniques listed in each category. In the determination to classify and categorize the various types of attacks in a logical and systematic order I was prompted to create the WEB OF KNOWLEDGE.

WEB OF KNOWLEDGE

The idea for the WEB OF KNOWLEDGE came to me twenty six years ago in Hawaii as I observed a spider constructing a web. As I watched the spider meticulously build this ingenious trap for his survival, I pondered the difficulties involved in learning the intricacies of the martial arts. Suddenly, I was struck with an idea. Could I not, from this perfect design, created by our Supreme Being, construct an intellectual trap; A trap that would aid in retaining Martial Arts knowledge? Surely, if one web could be constructed to ensnare victims, couldn't a similar one be devised to ensnare knowledge? As I began to develop the concept, I considered the topics that could be studied. What knowledge was the web to contain, and what order of priority would it follow? Would the topics of study vary from one belt level to another? If so, how should they be arranged? These as well as other unanswered questions made the going slow, but through perseverance, trial, and error, I arrived at this solution.

The Web is prioritized according to the degree of difficulty in handling an attack:

1. Grabs and Tackles — The beginning student should have a good chance against a grab, where the opponent does not instantly plan a punch. Without an immediate follow-up, a grab is basically inactive.

2. Pushes — Because of the forward momentum of pushes, they require more timing than grabs, but not as much as the required timing for a punch.

3. Punches — Still a greater degree of timing is required to defend against a punch, due to the faster speed and force of a punch.

4. Kicks — Not only do kicks require timing, but they have potentially greater power than punches — thus making them more dangerous.

5. Holds and Hugs — These in turn are more difficult because of the restriction of body movement and the limited number of available weapons and targets. There is a real danger of being taken to the ground.

6. Chokes and Locks — These are more dangerous than Holds and Hugs, as they have the potential of causing broken limbs and even instant death.

7. Weapons — The timing and power associated with weapons easily

rates them as being the most difficult to handle. Your opponent has a range advantage; with a high probability of serious injury or death.

8. Multiple Attacks Defense against multiple attacks requires skill and strategy. Being attacked by more than one opponent increases the probability of serious injury or death, and therefore, should be viewed as being equivalent to a single attacker well versed in the use of a weapon.

Careful examination of the techniques required in each of the belt levels will reveal that the topics listed above are in the exact order in which they are introduced to you. While all belt levels up through Green Belt follow the same sequence of topics, there are noticeable omissions of attack sequences. The omission of various attacks within the sequence may reflect the frequency with which different attacks occur. Lower belt requirements may stress more grabs, punches, hugs, or holds since there is a greater probability of encountering these types of attacks rather than kicking or weapons attacks. Secondly, beginners are not equipped to make the more difficult attack techniques work because of their limited experience.
Besides understanding the relative difficulty and danger of various attacks, you should explore related usages for the Web by visualizing and categorizing the various attacks according to direction, method, path, dimension, and angle of delivery or execution. For example, a punch might be delivered with a left or right hand, in a linear or circular motion, and while employing a variety of methods. Such methods of execution may:

> (1) create straight, hook, or roundhouse punches; (2) employ related methods in the form of a cross, jab, uppercut, chop, rake, or thrust type punches; (3) may require delivering punches with the rear or lead hand while in a stationary position, shuffling, or using a step through maneuver; or (4) by using combinations of any of the above. All methods of punching, grabbing, pushing, etc., and their combinations should be studied. The greater your knowledge of existing methods, the greater your repertoire of knowledge — all of which lessens your chances of being surprised. All motions that have been discussed may be compatibly inserted into the UNIVERSAL PATTERN.

In time you will learn that a specific technique used for a right hand grab may be suitably used for a right hand push or punch. It may require altering the timing of your action, but you, nevertheless, would still employ the identical technique pattern. When the structure of a technique allows for identical use against each of the types of linear motion mentioned, spontaneity is proportionately increased. There is no hesitation in deciding which technique to use, you simply respond to the action without deviating from the prescribed pattern. The substitution of a knife, however, would undoubtedly alter your technique pattern. Sophisticated strategy would be needed to control your opponent's actions. Naturally, logic should always dictate your need to alter, reduce, expand, or substitute your movements to increase your chances of success.

WEDGE - Triangularly shaped formation of body limbs which when employed can separate or force apart a two hand choke, grab, or push prior to countering.

WEIGHT DISTRIBUTION - The apportionment of weight related to a particular stance. It may vary, fifty-fifty, sixty-forty, ninety-ten, etc.

WHAT IF PHASE - This is PHASE II of the analytical process of dissecting a technique. This PHASE takes in additional variables. It requires being programmed to further analyze the IDEAL or fixed technique. Expected, as well as unexpected opponent reactions are projected and evaluated. The concept here is that every movement may have critical consequences; thus, in a realistic situation, the need to predict each consequence to the best of your knowledge is imperative. Ideally, all consequential possibilities should be projected, evaluated, and learned. To do so is to increase your ability to instinctively and randomly alter the basic technique, and thus allow yourself a choice of action.

WHEEL KICK - A type of kick resembling and paralleling the path of a ROUND-HOUSE KICK.

WHIP - A particular method of execution that employs a snapping type of blow or strike, but the magnitude of which has less force than a SNAP.

WHIPPING SLICE - See FLICKING SLICE.

WHITE-DOT-FOCUS - In this concept of focus one visualizes a white dot on a black background representing unawareness. All styles and systems that primarily stress linear motion conform to this concept. Their concern is with the target, and with maximizing power—not protection.

WHOLE - All functions of the mind and body acting as one.

WIDE KNEEL STANCE - This stance can stem from a NEUTRAL BOW AND ARROW STANCE by dropping the rear knee (about the length of your hand from the ground), and forcing it out. Your weight, at this point, should be evenly distributed (50-50). The drop in height can increase you stability, add power, help to avoid an attack, allow greater access to lower targets, and can be effectively used as a pin or check. The WIDE and CLOSE KNEEL STANCES obtain their names because of the differences in width, not in depth, that exist between them.

WIDTH DECEPTION - Conditioning your opponent to be accustomed to seeing a particular width of a stance or movement, and changing it without him being aware of it.

WIDTH ZONES - Synonymous with VERTICAL ZONES. This entails four vertical segments of the body that can be protected or attacked. See venitian blind concept.

WINDING - Rotating descent. Rotating of the body while gradually descending.

WINDMILLER - Tournament slang for one who continuously circles with his hands.

WINDSHIELD WIPER PRINCIPLE - Although similar to the SQUEEGEE PRINCIPLE, it differs in that one end is used as a pivot point. While both principles follow a path, the WINDSHIELD WIPER PRINCIPLE has one end remain in-place.

WING - A term used in self-defense techniques to refer to the elbow.

WITH - A very useful word in the Kenpo vocabulary, which is reserved for the more adept. It involves dual movements and eliminates the word "and". One doesn't block "and" then strike. He blocks "with" a strike. Employing this principle eliminates wasted motion and economizes on time.

WITHIN CONTACT - The second stage of the FOUR STAGES OF RANGE discussed in the DIMENSIONAL STAGES OF ACTION. This is the distance in which you or your opponent can be reached.

WORDS OF MOTION - Refers to a combination sequence of moves created by one arm or leg.

WORKING SEQUENCE - A technique sequence which is highly practical and applicable.

WRENCH(ING) - Execution of a violent twist/pull combination.

WRITING AND MOTION - The concept that writing and motion have similarities that can be paralleled. There are only three ways to write our language — print, cursive (script), and shorthand. Similarly, there are printed, cursive (script) and shorthand motions applied the hands and feet.

XYZ

YANK - To pull with vigor.

YIELD - To give way to your opponent's action. See RIDING.

YIN YANG SYMBOL - An ancient Chinese symbol. Yin represents the passive (the dark side of the symbol), Yang represents the active (the light side of the symbol). Together, they constitute equilibrium and harmony; everything has an opposite, but not in opposition. Instead, they are equally divided by a flexible line representing the continuity of life force which is movement.

YO YO - Tournament slang for one who continuously goes in and out without follow up techniques.

ZEN - Buddhist form of meditation perpetuated by Tamo (Daruma).

ZIG-ZAG - Following a series of diagonal paths by turning sharply at each angle change.

ZONE OF CONFINEMENT - Restricting your moves within certain imaginary boundaries or zones of space. Refer to CONTOUR CONFINEMENT.

ZONE CONCEPT - Same as ZONE THEORY.

ZONES OF DEFENSE - Same as ZONES OF PROTECTION.

ZONE DISCIPLINING - Controlling behavioral patterns through enforced obedience or physical compliance with the principles of the ZONE CONCEPT. Refer to CONTOUR DISCIPLINING.

ZONES OF OBSCURITY - See OBSCURE ZONES.

ZONES OF PROTECTION - This involves shielding three main zones on your body — height (or horizontal), width (or vertical) and depth. Also refer to OBSCURE ZONES, the OUTER RIM THEORY and the QUADRANT ZONE THEORY.

ZONES OF SANCTUARY - Dead areas of space where you can position yourself for protection. As an example, if we were to snugly fit a circle within a square we would find the corners of the square untouched. These untouched areas are called ZONES OF SANCTUARY, or areas outside the range of a natural weapon where one can take refuge, and not be touched. If the circle represented the path of a swinging club, taking refuge in the properly selected corner would prevent you from being hit. This area of refuge is therefore a ZONE OF SANCTUARY.

ZONE THEORY - This entails visualizing imaginary boundaries or zones of height, width and depth superimposed on your or your opponent's body. See DEPTH, HEIGHT, and WIDTH ZONES. It further involves OBSCURE ZONES, the OUTER RIM CONCEPT and the QUADRANT ZONE CONCEPT.

ZONE CONCEPT OF DIRECTIONAL MOVEMENT - This CONCEPT advocates eight accepted directional or linear paths which martial artists should follow when eluding, defending, or attacking an opponent. Like other zone theories, students are also encouraged to use their imagination to picture these directional paths on the ground, or upright (as if suspended in mid-air from the front, side, or back).

Notes

Notes

Index